The Down Syndrome Diary

JAMIE FREEMAN & FRIENDS

ISBN-13: 9798595955737 (paperback)

Cover design by: The Crimson Fox
Printed in the United States of America

Interior Photography by:

Sara Demick at www.sarademickphotography.com

&

Kelly Searle

Dedication

This book is dedicated to my beautiful boy, Benjamin James Freeman.
You made me a Mama, an advocate, a writer, and a better human being.

Thank you for opening my eyes to just how wonderful this world truly is.

Preface

The text in this book does not belong to any one individual. The entries were handwritten by twenty-six families over the course of seven years. The typed entries were edited as little as possible to maintain the integrity of the original author's written word.

You may find grammatical errors, language that isn't consistent with person-first language, or accepted vernacular in the disability community. We have chosen to keep these entries as written to show the vulnerability of our parents. All parents raising children with disabilities are on a journey to learn, grow, and change their perspectives.

We respect your journey and hope you respect ours.

Additionally, please keep in mind that each author is writing from one of four different countries. Each country has their own perspective on phrasing and word choice. An example of this is the term "Down syndrome." In the United States of America, we write and pronounce it as "Down syndrome." We capitalize and do not pluralize the "Down" and keep the word "syndrome" lower case. In the UK, they write and pronounce it "Down's Syndrome."

Additionally, you may find a lot of phrases and words in this book that are unfamiliar to you. For this reason, we have added an appendix at the end to assist the readers.

Sincerely,

The Down Syndrome Diary Authors

Foreword

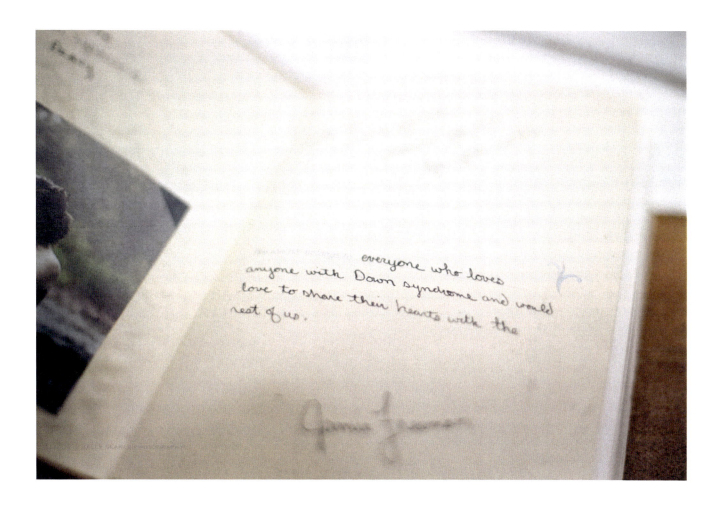

everyone who loves anyone with Down syndrome and would love to share their hearts with the rest of us.

Welcome to The Down Syndrome Diary! We are so glad you are here! Whether you have purchased this book to support new parents, or you are a new parent in our "club," we sincerely hope you enjoy the work of art you are about to experience.

First, I'd like to take the opportunity to give you a little backstory on this project. In 2013, I purchased that beautiful, leather-bound journal you see at the beginning of this foreword. Who am I? I am Jamie Freeman... mama to Benny. I purchased this journal with the intention of writing a letter to myself on the day I found out Benny would be born with Down syndrome. I just couldn't help but think how different that day would have been if I could have known what I knew six months later.

I have always had a love of pen & paper. I feel there's a rawness and an honesty to writing when there's no delete key. I kept journals my entire life until this point, and this was definitely a new chapter.

The project was born when I decided I wanted to share my diary. I found my peace with Benny's diagnosis when I found my now dear friend Tara's blog, Happy Soul Project. Learning about her daughter, Pip, made me see Down syndrome from the view of a parent instead of a doctor. Reading Tara's words gave me peace, and healing, so it only seemed fitting to ask her to write in it after me.

The rest was history.

Seven years after this moment, the diary came home to me. This living, breathing, work of art, filled with tears and wine stains, came back with a soul. This gorgeous little book had been shipped between twenty-six families, in four different countries! It had been held, cried over, and written in while living in the homes of everyone you are about to meet.

This diary traveled for seven years, and today it continues its journey as it has found its way into your hands.

Starting with the introduction all the way through the last entry, we have published the exact words from each writer. We edited only where absolutely necessary to maintain the integrity of each writer's story. We truly hope you enjoy reliving this journey with all of us. Pour yourself your own cup of whatever you prefer, sit back, relax, and get ready to embark on the journey of one little book with the goal of changing the world.

Lastly, if you just so happen to be one of the families I dreamed of when we started this project...someone who just found out they are inducted into the greatest club they never knew they wanted to be a part of...someone who just found out that your baby has been or will be born with Down syndrome...

CONGRATULATIONS!! You are in fantastic company!

Love,

Jamie Freeman

Introduction

May 2, 2014

Do you feel it? I can imagine it! I am the first to write in this book, so for now, it's just me and my horrible handwriting. But... I can't help but wonder how this book will feel in my hands when it makes its way back to me. This book will have had the hands of so many amazing people writing down their thoughts, fears, advice, suggestions and stories in it there is no way you'll feel inspired just holding it! So many mothers, fathers, sisters, brothers, friends, grandparents, aunts, uncles and more will have held this book. They will have laughed, cried, smiled, shook with bad memories, and became euphoric with happy ones.

This is my dream for this book.

If you are reading this book, then that means you have decided to go on this journey with me. Thank You!

Here are my instructions:

- Write your heart out!
- Write about anything pertaining to your loved one with DS or DS in general
- Start your entry with your name, date, and location
- Feel free to add a picture or two!
- Don't worry about your handwriting or scribbling things out. I think that's what will make this so special!
- Write as much, as little as you want!
- Please contact me to let me know you've received the book
- Tell others you have it and what it is! Use #thedownsyndromediary to post pics on Instagram or Twitter, or for Facebook comments
- Sent it on to the next family waiting to receive it. If you know someone that would be a good addition to the book just let me know and we can send it their way!
- I'll keep the order of who gets the book on my blog. I'll also have a map there documenting our journal's journey.

Have Fun. Be Honest. Be YOU!

Xoxo – Jamie

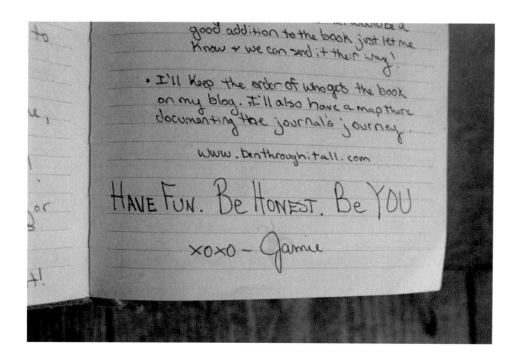

Jamie & Benny

"When these thoughts overwhelm me, I just think of my friends
in the DS community that have all been here before me."

—Jamie Freeman

Jamie Freeman
May 2, 2014
Dearborn, Michigan
USA

Benjamin James Freeman
8-5-2013

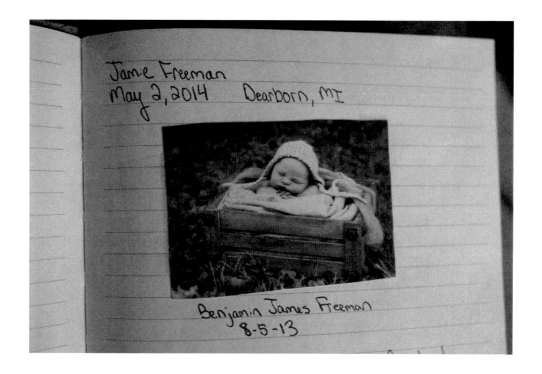

We had a pretty good idea that Ben had Down syndrome before he was born, but we weren't certain. We took a new blood test that was supposed to be 99% accurate and that came back positive. However, the doctors were all pretty skeptical considering they couldn't find any soft markers. My pregnancy began to feel like it was nothing but test after test. It was exhausting! Then, Ben was here. I can tell you that our lives are so much better because of that little dude!

As I'm writing this, I am sitting on my couch at the end of one of the worst weeks ever. We are REALLY blessed with Ben's health. He has no heart problems, eye problems, hearing problems and I even found out today that his thyroid is A-OK. Plus, at 8.5 months old, he had NEVER been sick. At least not until this week.

My poor guy came down with Strep Throat and Scarlet Fever. This resulted in an ER visit and two doctor visits this week. I have been a flipping hot mess! I literally did not sleep for three straight nights. I even fell asleep before work and slept through a conference call I was HOSTING! I have been an anxiety riddled, binge eating, sleep deprived, deadline missing mess – and it's only strep throat!

They tested Ben's blood cell count today to check for leukemia signs. I guess it's standard because of the fever and rash he had plus being at high risk for leukemia since he has Down syndrome.

This was the longest five minutes ever. He's fine. Blood Cells are good but come on! I can barely handle my poor guy's strep throat let alone leukemia! But… it could happen. A lot of things could happen.

When these thoughts overwhelm me, I just think of my friends in the DS community that have all been here before me. I think of their surgeries, and their ER visits. I realize, I can get through anything. I have support. I have friends, doctors, family, and my husband. I know I can do it. I have Ben. I will have Ben through it all and we will fight anything we need to. Whether it's laughing through his INSANELY stinky farts due to lactose intolerance, his severe hypotonia, or worse, we will smile our way through. After all, there was a time I would have said I wouldn't be able to handle a Down Syndrome diagnosis. Now, I consider it to be the greatest of ALL MY BLESSINGS!

(I apologize for my chicken scratch!)

Xoxo – Jamie

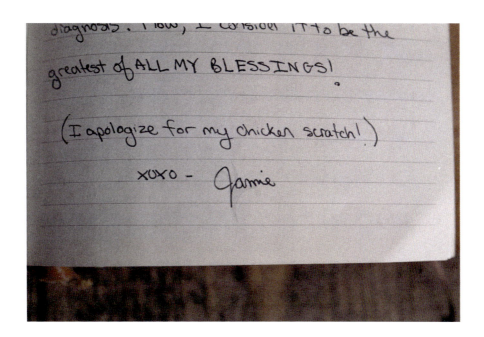

Tara & Pip

"What makes you different is what makes you beautiful."

—Tara Mccallan

Tara & Pip
Ontario, Canada
May 2014

Dear Momma,

When I was first asked to participate in The Down Syndrome Diary, I eagerly said yes. Little did I know that I would be the first person to write in it.

And it would take me months, to find the right words to express what was honestly in my heart.

Because, you see, I wish desperately I had this Diary to read the thoughts of other parents, when I found out my little girl Pip had Down syndrome.

I had a really hard go of it all.

When I found out I was having a little girl, I let my mind daydream to all I thought she would be.

Then three days after she was born, as we were about to be released from the hospital.

This Doctor looked at me with the saddest eyes, ones that will forever be burned in my memory.

And said, "I'm sorry to be the one to tell you this, but your daughter shows many signs of Down syndrome."

SLAP…

Right across the face – that's honestly what it felt like – I was so stunned.

Everything I ever hoped for my daughter, for my little family, seemed to die in that moment.

I've never wept like I did in that hospital bed – I was curled over literally shattered in devastation.

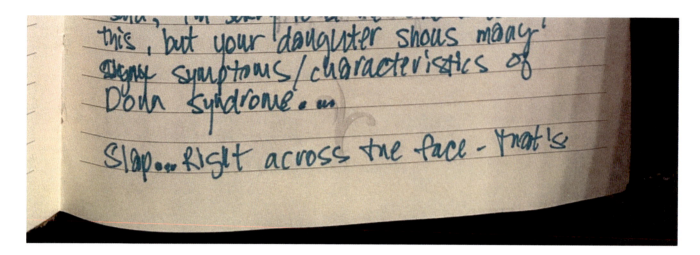

The following few days were a whirlwind of medical appointments to rule out complications associated with Down syndrome.

I couldn't tell you one bloody thing the Doctors said during that time.

All I remember is feeling the negativity that came from those meetings.

In one such "genetic counseling" appointment the Doctor went as far as saying, "For your next baby we can do testing and prevent this."

In the whirlwind, we were told that our daughter had congenital cataracts that needed immediate attention and a congenital heart defect.

In a way for me, this almost pushed Down syndrome to the side or up on the shelf to deal with later, as we prepared for surgeries, feeding tubes, months of heart failure, and finally heart surgery.

By the time we got through all that, taking Down syndrome back off the shelf to dust it off & deal with, didn't even need to happen.

It just became a part of Pip.
And a part I can honestly say I love and am feeling proud of.

It all changed for me when she had her first surgery at five weeks old.
Up until that point I hadn't physically said to anyone, "She has Down syndrome."
My way of dealing with it all was through words.
So, I started a blog called Happy Soul Project, in which my words were my healing grace in all of this.

But again, it's one thing to share behind a computer and another to be out in the world.
So, up until this point, I verbally had never said it out loud, but on this fated day I did.

I was down in the hospital gift shop, and a sweet old lady working behind the counter asked why I was there. To which I explained Pip's surgery and nervously added, "And she has Down syndrome."
It was as if by finally saying it out loud, it hit me.

Then, the sweet old lady dropped everything, came around the counter, put her hands on my shoulders, looked intently in my eyes and said,
"YOU ARE SO LUCKY!!!"

I didn't know what to think or say.
But, she continued and explained that her brother had Down syndrome.

Pip was on the cover of a national parenting magazine - the first model with special needs in over 30+ years.

And that he was absolutely the best thing in her life.
And made her who she was and kept their entire family together.
And you could see it in her face.
She meant every word.

And at that moment, I realized she was so right.
I had been looking at this all wrong.
Like I needed to learn to "accept" my daughter for her differences, when really I needed to learn how to celebrate and be changed by them.

In shifting my perspective, it has changed my life, and I'm sure the life Pip is going to have.
And I now feel like I'm that sweet old lady.
Wanting to wrap my arms around whoever needs to know's shoulders.
Sharing the secret that we are indeed, "THE LUCKY ONES".

I often think or wish there was a way I could go back and save all those tears I shed when I first found out.
However, I also think that grieving what you thought, gives room for expecting the unexpected. It's all a process that hopefully leads you to a love like no other.

A love that isn't in a diagnosis.

A love that can't even be understood, unless you get to experience life with a child who has Down syndrome.

So if you are reading this, you most likely are, welcome to the Club.

Love,

Tara – Pip's Lucky Momma

2021 Update:

Pip is the little girl who inspired the #differentisbeautiful movement & is the face behind the non-profit Happy Soul Project. She is now 8, loves music, annoying her brothers, & Doritos. She has the most contagious smile you've ever seen and her laugh seems to start in her toes. Pip made history and was the first child with special needs to be on the cover of a national parenting magazine here in Canada, was named the Canadian Down syndrome Hero of the Year and has had thousands of billboards up across the country to bring awareness & representation. Pip has been challenged with Type 1 Diabetes, Celiac Disease, Congenital Cataracts, double-knee-surgery, numerous heart defects, hypothyroidism, & other stuff, but it never stops her from changing every single person she meets.

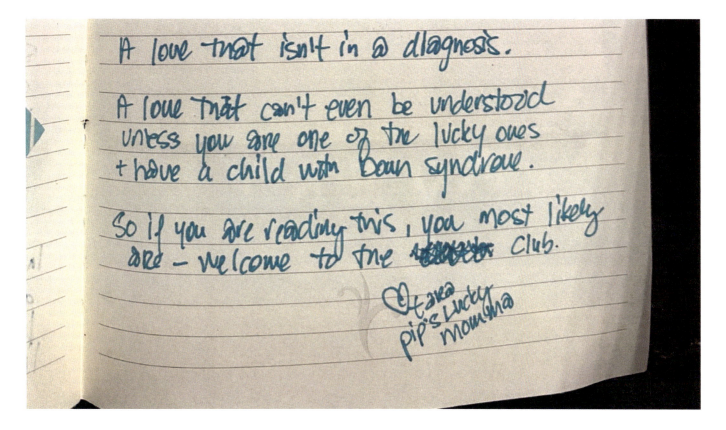

Helen & Avery

"Just know that your child will open your eyes to a new definition of 'special' and your life will be better than you could have ever imagined."

—Helen Lyn Morrison

Helen Morrison
Seattle, WA
September 2014

Avery was born April 9, 2012. My husband and I had been trying for a long time to conceive and after a very difficult miscarriage, we finally had what we'd always dreamed of – our precious baby boy! Nursing was quite difficult and as a result, he had a very hard time gaining weight. With much support and patience, we managed to nurse until he was eight months old. However, we began to notice that he was delayed in reaching his milestones, so at ten months old we had genetic testing done. We ended up finding out that Avery had Down syndrome one day after his first birthday.

I could fill pages and pages writing about what those thirty days felt like as we waited for his diagnosis, or how it seemed like my world stopped when I was told that my son had Down syndrome which could not be cured. However, I would rather write about what I have learned two and a half years later. The reality is that this journey amazes me everyday! I hope my words can give support and comfort to any parent with a new diagnosis.

When I first found out I would be contributing to this project, I thought long and hard about how I wanted to approach it. The one thing that has always stuck out in my mind has been how helpful other families have been and how their words have "carried me" along this journey. If the intent of this journal is to have our words and stories uplift new parents, then I would like to list some of the things I know to be true as a parent of a child with special needs.

Do not let your fear overwhelm you. When you first hear the words, "Your child has Down syndrome," tears will fall, your world will go silent, and sadness will overcome you. You may start your journey feeling fearful, but in time all you will feel is love and your worries will slowly evolve into a fierce sense of pride for your child.

Your child will crawl, walk, and run. It's ok to be impatient and to worry, but IT WILL HAPPEN! I wanted to see Avery crawl so badly I could taste it, and I was convinced he would never walk. Avery didn't crawl until he was sixteen months old and he just hit one of his biggest milestones yet – walking!! He began taking his first steps at twenty-seven months and now at twenty-nine months, he is full-blown walking! I can honestly say that I was so nervous that he would never walk. That may seem irrational to think, but learning to be patient between each big milestone is easier said than done. I think in our own way, we all struggle as we watch our children learn new things. It's ok to be anxious but just know THEY WILL DO IT ALL, just in their own time! I have learned to slow down and wait for "Avery Time."

Through our journey, I have noticed that people in my life have carried me through the good times and bad times, and they have done so in different ways. I can only speak for myself, but I have come to realize that a huge weight was lifted once I let go of some of my expectations and allowed others to support me in their own way.

There will be times when you lose patience. When you do, have the courage and strength to ask for help. I realize everyone's situation is different; however, sometimes reaching out to someone who can relieve you even for just an hour can be all you need. If someone offers to keep you company at a doctor's visit, say yes! I was fortunate and blessed to have my dad come to most of Avery's appointments. It meant the world to have someone to talk to while we ate or to take the stroller from me as I sobbed while Avery was attached to various cords (for tests). During those moments, it felt like I was going to "lose it" and having help saved me.

As I wrap up my small piece of this amazing diary – I want to leave you with these thoughts: Be kind to yourself and have faith that you are doing the best you can. Just know that your child will open your eyes to a new definition of "special" and your life will be better that you could have ever imagined.

You are never alone – welcome to this incredible community filled with ordinary people who have extraordinary children.

All my love,

Helen Morrison

Amy & Wesley

"Your worldview will never ever be the same and that's a good thing."

—Amy Thompson Knueppel

Amy and Wesley
Indianapolis, IN

November 2014

Hello Fellow Parent,

I am assuming that if you are reading this, you have received a pre- or post-natal diagnosis of Down syndrome. Let me be one of the first to tell you CONGRATULATIONS on your beautiful child and welcome to the DS family. We are so happy to have you on this journey with us.

We did not know Wesley had Down syndrome until 4 days after his birth. I had no markers on my ultrasounds and we elected not to do prenatal testing. Wesley was born at 36 weeks and 6 days. The NICU team was in the room because he was a preemie (by 1 day)! They noticed he was a little "floppy" but otherwise well. He was able to breastfeed right away and was only in the NICU because he had jaundice.The words Down syndrome weren't even mentioned until a nurse thought she heard a heart murmur. They did an echocardiogram which was negative for any heart issues but the team began to pay closer attention to Wesley.

The diagnosis was delivered by a doctor I'd never seen before. My husband was home with our daughter so I was by myself when I heard the news. I sobbed as I felt all the dreams I had for my son shatter into a million pieces. He would not be a soccer or basketball star. He wouldn't go away to college. He wouldn't get married. I was beside myself.

I called my sister, who is a Child Life Specialist at a hospital in another state, to tell her about Wesley's diagnosis. What she said next shocked me. She took a breath and said, "Aim, I loved him before, but I love him 500 times more now." My first thought was, "Why? How is that possible?!"

Oh how I wish I knew then what I know now.

I wish I knew how much joy Wesley would bring our family and the world around him. I wish I knew how he would brighten others' days with a wave and a smile (especially for pretty ladies)! Aside from the wonder that is Wesley, I wish I knew that I would meet so many other amazing families, both online and in real life. We have a group of over 100 moms here in Indy who all have young kids with Down syndrome. We call ourselves "The Lucky Ones."

Please, give yourself time to mourn, time to feel angry, overwhelmed, sad, desperate, and anything you need to feel. Let those feelings wash over you as long as you need to. It took me a while to be able to say, "My son has Down syndrome." I worried about the stigma or that people would be ugly. Boy was I wrong. It seems that so many people have a connection to Down syndrome and ALL of them have had nothing but positive things to say. I have had people stop me in stores to tell me about their "blessing" with Down syndrome who is in his 20's or 30's. Or about their uncle, cousin, neighbor who has DS and has been the brightest spot in their lives.

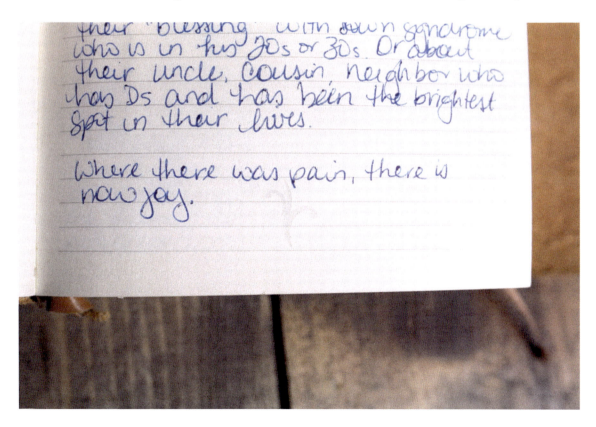

Where there was pain, there is now joy. Your child will spur you on to be an advocate. He/she will teach your family to slow down and appreciate the small moments. We took so many things for granted that we now celebrate. We have full-on screaming, clapping, parties over milestones such as sitting up, pulling to stand, and signing words.

Build a team that believes in your child. Seek out therapists that see your child's potential. We had a PT (physical therapist) tell us that Wesley would never walk and our hearts broke. We closed that door, found a new PT, and I am happy to report that at 27 months, we can hardly get him to sit down because he is walking everywhere!

It is not all unicorns and rainbows. There are days that I hate having Early Intervention Therapy 3x/week. There are times where I wish Wesley would do x, y, or z. But he'll do something else that will make me think, "Oh, not in my time and not according to my wishes."

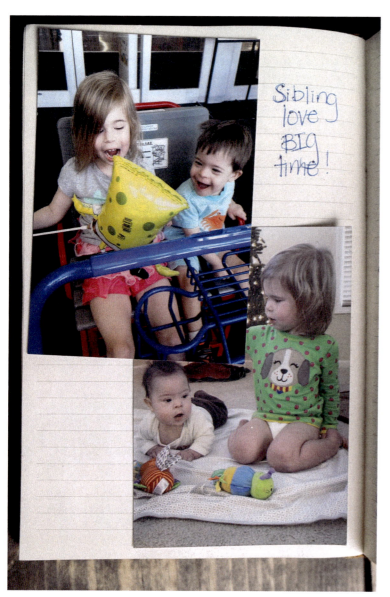

I think Wesley has opened our eyes to the amazing in the ordinary. He has allowed us to see that differences make the world more beautiful and that people who are "different" can make this world brighter. We became aware that children with Down syndrome and other special needs are being abandoned all over the world because they aren't perfect. Knowing this, our family has decided to adopt a child with special needs internationally. Crazy, right? Something that was so scary is now something we see as a blessing.

Enjoy your child! Don't listen to the people (including doctors) who say, "Your child will never do_____ because of Down syndrome." Just sit back and marvel at what your child will do. Learn your child's strengths and play to them. If that means playing Taylor Swift and Katy Perry to get him to walk, do it (not that I am speaking from experience there).

I love this quote as it relates to DS and the things you may hear:

> "Listen to the mustn'ts, child.
> Listen to the don'ts.
> Listen to the shouldn'ts, the impossibles, the won'ts.
> Listen to the never haves, then listen close to me…
> Anything can happen child.
> Anything can be."
>
> —Shel Silverstein

As I have lived this life, I can tell you with honesty:

- Your child will bring you immeasurable joy
- Your child will teach you to appreciate and celebrate the small things
- Your child will teach you that all people have beauty and that differences make the world a better place
- Your world view will never ever be the same and that's a _good_ thing
- You will learn to fight for the underdog and champion those who have no voice
- You will be grown, stretched, and become a you that you never thought possible

Much Love!
Amy Knueppel

And a P.S. – Your other childrens' lives will be enriched and blessed because of their siblings! Vivian _loves_ her brother. She is his biggest cheerleader. She is kinder and more compassionate because of him. She loves to help with therapies and therapy homework. Despite her love, they are still siblings and they can fight and argue like anybody else can.

who have no voice
- you will be grown, stretched, and
become a you that you never
thought possible.

Cheers to your amazing journey!
Much love!
Amy Knueppel

Steve & Valkyrie

"I know it may seem like the world is collapsing around you. I know that it all seems unfair, but I assure you that everything is going to work out."

—Steve Ferguson

Steve Ferguson
St. George, Utah, USA

I sit here alone now, with only the sounds of my pugs snoring to keep me company, reading *The Down Syndrome Diary* and watching Valkyrie toss and turn on the baby monitor. As I read the previous parents' chapters, I smile with their stories of achievement and weep with the all too familiar stories of confusion and sorrow after receiving the Dr.'s diagnosis. I will be the 5th author to tell their story in this amazing book. As I sit with pen in hand, I can't help but think; somewhere in the world is a twenty-something year old future parent who has no idea that a child with Down syndrome is in their future. And when they do finally get this news, whether that be in a couple of years or many, my words could potentially bring them comfort in a time when they are going through thoughts and feelings that only a special needs parent can understand and relate to. I hope that these words will help calm their minds and let them see that DS is nothing to fear or cry about and that this book is full of amazing success stories of families who have embraced and thrived with Down syndrome in their lives!

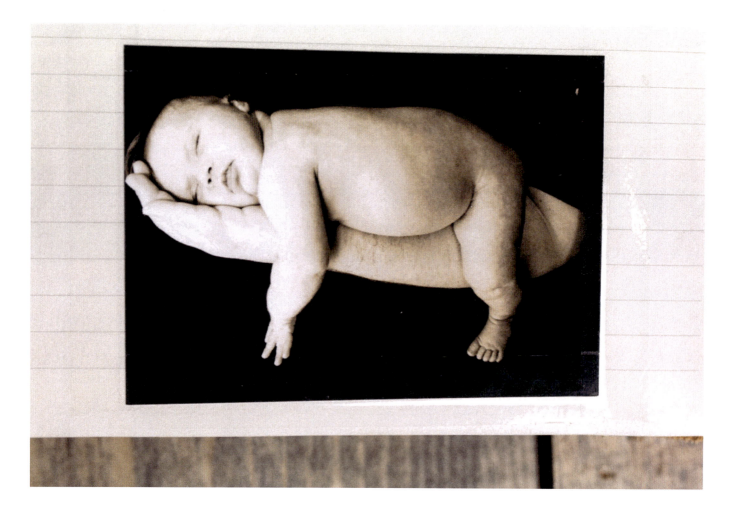

Time to write my chapter…

January 2015

"About Me and The Diagnosis"

My name is Steve Ferguson. I am 28 years old and live in St. George, Utah with my wife of 8 years, Charla. We got married young, at 19 and 20, and always said we'd wait until the right time to have children…You know, that time when you both have perfect careers and a big beautiful home, and you're completely financially sound. Yeah haha. As I'm sure you know you can never truly be prepared for a baby! Well in 2012, I began to get very "Baby Hungry." I didn't even know men could feel this way, and certainly didn't think I would ever truly WANT a baby! It took us quite a while to finally get pregnant. Charla was on the birth control shot, and it seemed to take a long time to finally wear off. When I found out she was pregnant, I was ecstatic! I immediately began to plan my son's future (of course it would be a boy). I had visions of a little mini-me, only a toddler, but still managing to have a great beard and mohawk like Daddy, walking down the street in matching clothes! When we went to the doctor and found

out my son was actually a daughter, I was admittedly disappointed. As my grandfather told me a while back, "No pressure, but if you or your brother don't have a son, the Ferguson name dies with you." Now I know there are thousands of Ferguson families out there, but our particular branch is relying on us, and so far we are failing LOL. My brother has 2 daughters, and I have got Valkyrie. So we're still working on it! I got over the fact that V would be a girl quickly and was still stoked that I would be a Daddy soon! In the following ultrasound we would be given the terrifying news that our baby had a potential heart defect, which would send us down a 6 month path that I blame my currently 25% grey hair on! We were sent to a Fetal Heart Specialist who was the first person to suggest the possibility of our baby having Down syndrome. He said that heart defects are very common with people with DS and Valkyrie also had a "white spot" on her heart in the ultrasound that was also a marker for DS. Now, we had already done the usual blood tests at the OB that could tell you if your baby had any genetic issues, and all those tests came back negative, so I wasn't that worried about it. Two weeks later we received a call from the Heart Specialist's office asking us to come in so they could talk to us about the test results.

Before I continue, I have some things about myself that I'm ashamed of but must admit to you…

Like most people, I have many fears: spiders, sasquatch, etc. But my biggest fear in life, a fear most would describe as irrational. I was terrified of having a child with disabilities, more specifically mental disabilities. As I went through my twenties, this fear grew larger as the reality of having children got closer. I remember making remarks to friends that I'd rather just adopt a child than have my own and risk it being mentally handicapped. This fear eventually grew into a phobia for me. Before my wife and I got married in 2006, she was working at a group home for women with mental disabilities. I remember (please try not to hate me) asking her to shower before coming to my apartment when she'd get off work. Disgusting, I know. The fact that she stayed with me shows what an amazing and understanding woman she is! Now understand, I was never cruel to or hated people with disabilities, I was just completely ignorant. I was never exposed to anyone with mental disabilities as a child and always felt uncomfortable around them. In high school, I remember trying to avoid the kids from the special needs class in the hallways. I just had no idea how to interact with them, didn't know what to say or how to act. I remember being told "hello" by some and just pretending not to hear them. As I write these words, I feel ashamed of my past ignorance to those with special needs. So that's a little history about my mindset toward mental disabilities and fears of having a child with them.

Back to the phone call from the doctor's office. Another thing about me is, I am a massive pessimist. I always expect the worst and plan for the worst! So naturally, when we received this phone call, my heart sank. The days leading up to the meeting with the doctor, I was a complete nervous wreck. My wife, who is always optimistic, was even nervous. I remember walking into the room at the doctor's office… I can't stress to you enough how small this room was! The average walk-in closet is bigger! I'm a big dude, and I remember squeezing into a chair between the round table in the room and the wall. I could feel my heartbeat throughout my entire body, even my vision would blur with each beat. The doctor walked in and the first thing he said, with sorrow in his eyes was, "Well obviously I wouldn't have called you in here if I had good news." My heart stopped, my mind went blank, I felt my skin heat up as blood rushed to it, and I became bright red. "Your baby has Down syndrome…" It had happened… My worst fear, my "irrational fear" had come true. Instantly, my wife and her mom and sister, who had come for moral support all looked at me, knowing that this was my biggest fear. I remember my mother-in-law holding my hand under the table. I couldn't squeeze back. I don't

remember much of what the doctor said after that. He pulled out a few pieces of paper with charts of squiggly X's on them and I heard the word chromosome a few times, and then he left. As we waited for a Genetic Counselor to come in, my sister-in-law said it all made sense. My wife was great with people with special needs and that God had sent her one. I remember snapping back at her, "This has nothing to do with God. It's just a random occurrence!" That was the only thing said while we waited. I later apologized to her. The Genetic Counselor came in and within the first 2 minutes, said she could help arrange an abortion if that's the direction we wanted to go. She spoke for a while longer, answering the girls' questions. She then nervously asked me if I was OK. I can't imagine what I must have looked like. I told her I needed to go. She instantly got up and held the door open so the others could quickly exit the room before the 300 lb. ape (me) exploded in the small room. On the drive home, I don't remember much, but I do remember my wife telling me I could leave. She said I could leave her and she'd understand. She'd let me go. Obviously my parents raised me better than that, and it was never an option for me! Abortion was also out of the question. I felt trapped… I knew I couldn't be a POS and abandon my wife and unborn child, and I knew I couldn't live with myself knowing I'd murdered my own baby. My only option was to "man-up" and accept the hand I was dealt.

After spending a few days feeling sorry for myself, I took to the internet to better understand what the future and this baby had in store for me. After reading the Wikipedia page on Down syndrome and a few others that were published by doctors, I wanted to find actual parents to talk to, actual people who have been in my shoes that could offer me some advice. Facebook quickly became my refuge! I found several pages and groups that were full of parents who wanted nothing more than to help me. A couple to be specific were "Kids With Down Syndrome" and "Fathers of Children with Down Syndrome – Band of Brothers." On these pages and many others, I read stories and saw photos and videos of what appeared to be happy families and VERY happy children with DS! I instantly began to feel better about my situation. Seeing all these other fathers proudly showing off their kids on social media made me feel like my life wasn't over, and I wasn't alone. Finally one afternoon, I posted a simple question to one of the pages, "I recently found out my unborn daughter has Down syndrome. Is there anything I need to do differently to prepare for her coming into our lives?" The page shared my question on their wall, and within 24 hours, I had received over 600 answers from parents of children with

DS from all over the world! The number one answer I received was, "You don't need to do anything differently, just prepare to feel the most overwhelming feeling of love you'll ever know." And they were 100% correct!

"Meeting Valkyrie"

After coming to terms with the fact that Valkyrie would have DS, we focused on her heart condition. We were sent to Primary Children's Hospital in Salt Lake City, where a heart specialist told us that we didn't need to worry about her heart! We were ecstatic! Charla had a great pregnancy and actually worked all the way until her water broke ... at work! She insisted from the beginning that she wanted a drug free birth, and she did it. After 13 hours of labor, Valkyrie June Ferguson came into our lives at 9lbs. 1oz., big girl (also very uncharacteristic for babies with DS.) On that note: DO NOT pigeon hold your child with DS to ANY of the standards that your doctor or books may tell you. Valkyrie has pretty much shattered every expectation that doctors, books, or we have put on her. Since the test that came back positive for DS was only 95% accurate, when V was born, the doctor placed her on my wife's chest and said to the several nurses in the room, "What do ya think?" Asking if she looked like she had DS. We all confirmed in unison with a "Yep."

Just remember that people with Down Syndrome can pretty much learn anyth we can, it just takes longer, patienc and persistence are key! Valkyrie.s

She had those beautiful almond shaped eyes and tiny bridgeless nose. After they got her all cleaned up, one of the nurses also showed me another marker, the single crease across the palm of her hand. To this day, I still don't understand how having an extra chromosome would do that, but it's fun to show people. Just as the parents on Facebook had predicted, I fell instantly in love with this little girl! Her little tongue slightly protruded out of her mouth, and she looked right into my eyes, casting a spell on my heart. We stayed at the hospital for 3 days because V had a little case of jaundice, unrelated to DS, and required one of those baby tanning beds. We took her home and like most parents, didn't sleep for about 3 months straight! The only thing V having Down Syndrome really affected was breast feeding. Generally babies with DS have low muscle tone which can affect their ability to suckle and their large tongue can also get in the way. This was the case with V. So Charla pumped, and we bottle fed. Otherwise, everything was "normal" except the fact that our baby was cuter than everyone else's!

I can't believe Valkyrie will be one next week! Time really does fly by once you have children! She has done so well this year. She's in physical therapy or "Early Intervention" which I can't recommend enough. It's another one of the things that I would have never known about had I not been on social media asking questions. She has kept up with all the milestones that "typical" children should be hitting at certain ages. She's great at army crawling but hasn't quite figured out how to get up on her knees, but we continue to work with her. One of the most important things to remember about Down syndrome is that every individual person learns at their own pace! Never feel discouraged if another child with DS is walking or talking before yours. They all have their strengths and weaknesses, just like us. Just remember that people with Down syndrome can pretty much learn anything we can, it just takes longer. Patience and persistence are key! Valkyrie says 3 words now: Mom, Dada, and Pups when she sees dogs. Everyone who spends time around her tells us we are spoiled because of her VERY happy demeanor. She smiles at anyone who smiles at her and is probably a bit too friendly with strangers and really has no problem being picked up by anyone! I've struggled going to church over the years, but the LDS (Mormons) have been amazing to Valkyrie and our family! We joke that V thinks people gather at church to worship HER. They have treated her like a celebrity since she was born. As several people in our ward, including our Bishop, have family members who have DS. The church even gave us $900 to help pay for half of Valkyrie's helmet (which I'll touch on in a minute). I've never been strong in the church like my wife, but I'll continue to go because it's so important to me that V has them as a support system. Who knows, maybe I'll finally learn a thing or two.

When V was born, she was stuck in the birth canal for about 20 minutes and developed a hematoma (a 5 inch bump on the back of her head). As a result, she slept on the right side of her head for the first few months, and her head began to grow misshapen. She was prescribed an Orthotic helmet to reshape her head. She's been wearing it for about 5 months, and it's made a huge difference! She should only need to wear it for a few more months. Had she not gotten the helmet, she ran the risk of losing the vision and hearing on one side of her head because her brain would push against the skull, on top of having an odd shaped head. Our insurance refused to cover it so we had to pay $1800 for it! So make sure your kids don't sleep on just one side of their heads. This was also unrelated to DS, just new parents who didn't know any better. We did run into one speed bump associated with DS a few months ago. We did another echocardiogram on her heart, which is recommended with kids with DS after birth. It turns out she has a small heart defect. It's called an Atrial Septal Defect (ASD), a small hole between the top two chambers of heart. As of now, the doctors aren't worried about it! She had an EKG done, and the heart is working just fine. The hole will most likely close on it's own, but if surgery is required, it won't be for a few years. It can be repaired via catheter through the artery in her leg, so no open heart surgery! But enough talk about that stuff. Despite it all, Valkyrie is such

*In September 2014 we did our first Buddy Walk! Team Valkyrie raised over $1,000 and had 40+ members. We even got corporate sponsorship from a mortgage Co.

my wife was working for at the time and got team shirts! We highly recommend doing BuddyWalks!*

a fun happy little girl. Her absolute favorite food is Ice Cream! I have to constantly yell at her mom not to feed it to her. For her birthday next week, we are having an ice cream bar with all the toppings!

Before I did my research and understood what Down syndrome really was, I thought my daughter would just be...kind of a vegetable. Not really responding to the world around her, not having a connection to her family. I saw myself having to change her diaper for the rest of my life. All I could think about was how it would negatively affect my future. I'd never get to retire because I'd always have to take care of her financially. In my experience and research, men in general seem to have a more difficult time accepting that their child has or will have Down syndrome. We have an almost primal expectation that we will have genetically perfect and superior children...they will be better than all others. I grew up being strong, intelligent and artistic, and I expected that my children would be the same. In my mind, I figured I'd have a couple of these "superior children," and after 20 years they would move out, and I'd be free again to retire and live out the rest of my days vacationing. Hearing that my daughter would have Down syndrome completely obliterated every single idea of what I thought my life would be like. Granted, she is only one year old, but I know that all my fears about the future were completely ridiculous! I now know that people with DS can go on to live completely normal lives. My Bishop's brother, Layne Johnson, was born with Down syndrome nearly 60 years ago, at a time when very little was known about DS. He was medically diagnosed as having "Mongolism" (now, a very derogatory term for Down Syndrome). It was recommended to his parents that he be placed in an institution because he would never have the ability to think, let alone live any shadow of a normal life. To demonstrate, they held up a small statue of an elephant and said that he'd never be capable of identifying that it was an elephant or even be able to distinguish it from a real elephant! Well fast forward 60 years and Layne has retired from JCPenny where he worked for 30 years. He has been married to his wife Shauna (who also has DS) for 20 years and has maintained an accident-free driving record for over 30 years! Does that sound like someone who belonged in an institution? We were lucky

give myself a hug and assure him that his life isn't over. Tell him that in a few months he will meet the love of his life and everything will work out! These kids have a power, something we all see but don't understand, a power to make you smile, to make you fall in love.

enough to have Layne participate in Valkyrie's blessing in church. It meant so much to me to have someone who has so inspirationally risen above Down syndrome be there to help bless my daughter! I no longer worry about how Valkyrie having Down syndrome will negatively affect my life...I'm too busy enjoying the MANY positive aspects!

"My Advice to You!"

After all the help and support I received from social media, family and friends, and church members, I now make a huge effort to help anyone who is in the same position I was 18 months ago. I seek out questions from new parents on social media, give out my information to anyone in my community who approaches me about their friend or family member who just found out their baby has DS, and I've started to volunteer in a local Down syndrome group, The Southern Utah Down Syndrome Association. Last month I was on the board that organized the yearly Christmas party and ran the cake walk game. I had a blast watching all the kids play the game and handing out cupcakes! It's truly bizarre how dramatically I've changed over the past year. I went from being terrified of those with mental disabilities to organizing an event being surrounded by them and having a great time, never one awkward feeling! Recently I saw a post on a page asking parents, "If you could go back and give yourself advice to help deal with the diagnosis that your child has Down syndrome, what would you say?" Well this is what I'd say to myself and the advice I give to any future parents who may be reading this...

Your little angel, that beautiful baby, is going to be okay! YOU are going to be okay! I know it may seem like the world is collapsing around you. I know that it all seems unfair, but I assure you that everything is going to work out. It's ok to cry, it's ok to feel overwhelmed. We all did! But don't be sad, please don't be sad and don't be afraid. I can't stress to you enough that Down syndrome is nothing to fear or feel sorrow over. I wasted so much time feeling sorry for myself, neglecting the feelings of my wife, so focused on how this would negatively affect my life. I wish I could go back and just give myself a hug and assure him that his life isn't over. Tell him that in a few months, he will meet the love of his life and everything will work out! These kids have a power, something we all see but don't understand, a power to make you smile, to make you fall in love. The innocence and purity of their soul radiates throughout them and spreads to all who come in contact with them. I don't know if we have been chosen by a higher power to be the caretakers of these special souls, or if it all is just random…I'm just glad that it was out of my control. Because I would have never chosen to have a child with Down syndrome, but I'm thankful everyday that it wasn't up to me! Valkyrie has changed my life. Her smile reminds me daily that none of the small stuff I worry about means anything. Her eyes tell me that she loves me, and I know that that's all I'll ever need in this life. I say that I'm her caretaker…but I often wonder if she was sent here to be mine.

The Ferguson Family
Steve, Charla, and Valkyrie

2021 Update: Valkyrie is now age 7 and has 4yr old twin sisters Rae & Sloan and a 3yr old brother Harvey!

Follow our story on Instagram:
@steveferg

Email: steve.ferg.86@gmail.com

The Ferguson Family
Steve, Charla & Valkyrie

Follow our story on Instagram:
@steveferg

Email: steve.ferg.86@gmail.com

Kelly & Dolly

"I will cry, but I will RISE ABOVE!"

—Kelly Searle

Kelly and Dolly
Pittsburgh, PA
March 2018

DOLLY

Dolly Ryan Searle
Born: June 27th, 2013 Pittsburgh, PA
Meaning of Dolly: "Gift of God"

My name is Kelly Searle, and I am a mom of six children! Yes, that's right! It was a blended marriage for myself and my husband. We each brought two kids into our marriage and have two together. Our littlest girl, Dolly, has Down syndrome. She was born in June of 2013.

It was a pretty normal pregnancy, but at 20 weeks we received a call from our doctor that they had found a marker for Down Syndrome in her heart. They wanted us to get further testing done, but we declined. It wouldn't have changed anything so we decided to enjoy the rest

of our pregnancy. We pushed the idea that she had Down syndrome far back into our heads to the point where we didn't believe it. We never spoke of it again. Thinking back now, I think that we were both too terrified to speak of it because that would make it real.

Fast forward 4 months and our beautiful girl found her way into this world. It was a pretty easy labor and delivery but what followed was some of the most painful moments of the birth experience. The words that follow are as truthful and raw as I can be with you. The second they handed me my newborn daughter, I knew she was different. I saw it in her eyes, in her face, and the way she was looking at me. I knew instantly in my heart without any doubt of certainty. I still don't know why, but I kept quiet. I whispered to her, "I love you just the way you are." I held my breath and kept waiting for someone else to acknowledge she has Down Syndrome. Nobody said anything. Not my husband, not a nurse, not a doctor...not a soul. I began to think that I was awful for thinking that my daughter had Down Syndrome. I finally got up enough courage to say something to my husband. "Does she look different to you?" I asked him. Praying that he would see it too, but also praying that it wasn't true. For hours, we would sit in the hospital room that night Googling "What do babies with Down syndrome look like?" It all became a blur. My husband was convinced that I was imagining things, and it wasn't true. We kept quiet all night, and I just kept whispering to her over and over again, "You are perfect just the way you are." I couldn't stop kissing her. It was like it was our little secret between my new little girl and myself. The next morning, God would decide that it was time for the whole world to know our secret.

It was around 9 am, the day after Dolly was born. My husband started to notice that our little girl was turning blue. We called a nurse in to check on her. At that time, my husband finally blurted it out to the nurse, "Does our baby look like she has Down syndrome to you?" This was the moment the path of my entire life was about to change.

She was a sweet older nurse. I remember how carefully she examined Dolly's feet, the palms of

her hands, and her eyes so softly and gently the entire time. She looked at us and said, "I'm so sorry, but I think it's a strong possibility she does have Down syndrome." The series of events after that are ones that will forever be etched into my brain just as fresh as if they just happened. My husband immediately broke down into tears. I had never in my life seen him cry so hard. I held him as he sobbed into my chest. I was unable to cry at that moment. I wanted to be strong for my husband, and after all, my daughter had already told me her secret the night before.

The next hours were full of doctors speaking about works like "retardation" and discussing the things my daughter would never do. On top of that, Dolly had some heart issues that put her in the NICU. There was a valve in her heart that never closed and they discovered a hole in her heart. Seeing my daughter, my helpless new baby, hooked up to so many machines and

"BIG BROTHER"

FAMILY MOMENTS

DOLLY EATING CAKE ON HER 1ST BDAY WITH HER SISTERS

JOY

TONGUE PROTRUSION: SOMETHING THAT I ONCE FEARED IS NOW SOMETHING THAT I EMBRACE ABOUT MY LITTLE GIRL. I NOW KISS HER WHEN SHE DOES IT.

THINGS I LOVE ABOUT YOU

★ HOW could you resit that smile↑? ★

knowing that her little heart was "broken" sent me into a complete breakdown. I finally cried. I sobbed uncontrollably. That ugly kind of cry that leaves you unable to speak and makes you almost too weak to walk.

I need you to know something in case it can help you the way it helped us. My husband and I did NOT go to church every Sunday. We still do NOT go to church every Sunday, but after Dolly was born my husband found the little old chapel inside of our hospital. He would go down there by himself and pray for us. He would kneel down and beg God to heal our little girl. He would pray for God to give him peace and to give me comfort. He would cry his heart out a couple of times a day in that tiny little chapel. He would then come up to my room and place his entire body over me and pray over me. I would bury my head into his chest and sob. He would kiss my head over and over again. He held me so tight and so protective while he prayed that I felt like he and God were carrying me through what was happening. He would pray over our daughter. He would place his big strong hands over our daughter's tiny little chest and pray for God to fix her heart. We would do this several times a day. I started to go to the chapel with him and pray with him. We would always pray for the same things: to heal Dolly's heart, for comfort, for a peace to go over us, and for the babies and other parents in the NICU to find peace and be healed. The hardest part of everything was having to be discharged from the hospital and our little girl having to stay there in the NICU.

Something beautiful began to happen to us. We started to find peace and comfort. We forgot about Down Syndrome and just wanted her heart to heal. And it did! It healed itself. It would also heal itself three months later when a hole in her tiny heart closed. My daughter amazes me every day, surprises me every day...and her heart healing itself was just the beginning.

Why are you here? Why are you reading this? If you have recently received a diagnosis, I just want to be the first to tell you CONGRATULATIONS! You have become a chosen one. Your child has chosen YOU to be their parent. God felt that YOU were lucky enough to become a part of an important exclusive club. You are a lucky one. Your whole life is going to change for the better. Your life is going to be enriched in ways you've never imagined.

First, I know you are scared. I am too. We will get through this together though. All of those dreams and things you've imagined for your child, they were yours, not theirs. It is okay to mourn them though. I still mourn things almost daily. But that is OKAY. Our children will still do great things...but it will be THEIR things. Their dreams, their goals, their joys in life. Dolly's personality has already come out. If she doesn't want to do something, she lets me know. I listen to her. I follow her lead. I let her tell me what she can handle. I don't force her. She teaches me more than I could have ever imagined. I have learned more about patience and slowing down in the past 2 years than I have my entire life. She makes me better. She makes my husband better. She makes our kids better. She makes us love harder, enjoy life more and reminds us not to take things for granted. We should all slow down and enjoy life the way our kids do. Why are we in such a hurry?

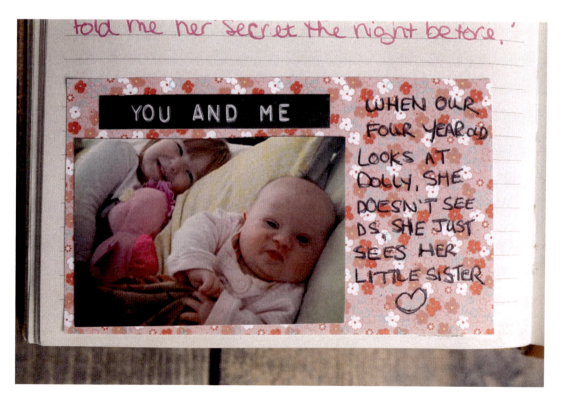

I can honestly say that I see more of a sense of wonder in Dolly than I ever did with our other kids. She studies everything closely and slowly. She is intrigued and curious about everything. She is like a little sponge. She soaks everything in and stores it in that tiny, cute head of hers. When she is ready, she uses it. It takes her a little longer to say words and it took her a little longer to walk. She took her first step at 16 months. Today, I can honestly say, at 20 months, she is trying to RUN across the house and gets into absolutely EVERYTHING she can.

That's the wonder of our kids. If your child doesn't walk at 16 months, or 20 months, or even 24 months – DO NOT WORRY! They will. On their own time, when they are ready. They have soaked it all in, and they will let it out when they are ready. What's the hurry? Take a look at that smiling face looking up at you. Is it really so bad that we get to carry our babies around a little longer?

Some days are still rough. It's okay to talk to someone about those days. It's not all unicorns and rainbows. I allow myself to cry. I get sad sometimes, and I spend a lot of time

worrying. My biggest struggle is that my little girl will never have children of her own. I get sad when I think about her watching her older sisters and brother grow up and get married. She'll watch them have kids and have families of their own. I don't want her to long for a baby of her own. It is something that I struggle with all the time. My other kids remind me though that their kids one day are going to love "Aunt Dolly," and she will probably be their favorite.

I started joining local support groups in my area when she was about a year old. I am happy to say that Dolly has already made a ton of "boyfriends" at the ripe old age of almost two! 😃 This has brought me peace. I want her to get married one day (if she wants to!). I think that it's important for her to be surrounded by a Down Syndrome community. We have playdates and get-togethers. I even met one of my dearest best friends through a support group. Her little boy has Down syndrome. The second we started talking, it was like I knew her my whole life. God chose to bring us together for a reason. She is teaching me lessons, and I am teaching her. All of this because Dolly chose ME to be her mom! All of these wonderful people in our life that we would have otherwise never met.

My husband and I believe that this is all intentional. He thinks that Dolly was brought into our lives to save our souls. We have both used hurtful words in the past, words that I'm so ashamed to admit. I am embarrassed that I never took the time before Dolly to think of how hurtful certain words can be. My entire family are now advocates for celebrating individuals that may be a little different. We try to push the concept that to be different is beautiful! It is not scary, and it should not be kept silent!

The past few weeks have been very hard for me. We are having some struggles with another child of ours that doesn't have Down syndrome. Because I have gone through what I have with Dolly, I sometimes want to have self-pity or say "Why me?" My husband is always quick to snap me out of it and remind me that life is meant to be LIVED and not kept quiet. I am cherishing each day and will rejoice in the blessings before me.

We are the lucky ones.

★REPEAT WITH ME★

I will rise above.
I will stay strong.
I will slow down.
I will have patience.
I AM STRONG.
MY DOLLY IS STRONG.

I will cry, but I will RISE ABOVE.

"Daddy loved you so much he decided to give you an extra one of his chromosomes. That is why you are so special." – My husband when my daughter was a week old.

—Kelly 🩷

To follow me and connect, visit me on Instagram @everly_kelly_searle

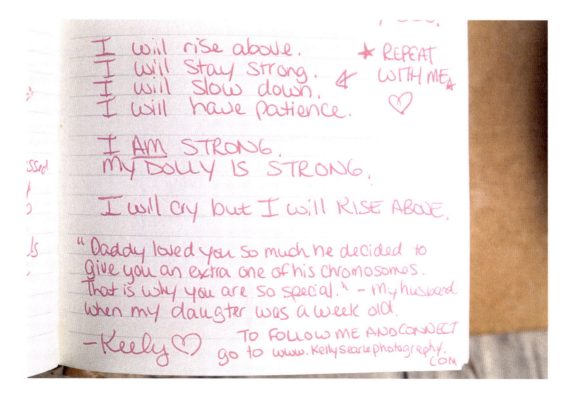

Kimberly & Mia

"She is so very strong, and has made us so happy
with her tenacity and fighting spirit."

—Kimberly Cheeseman

Mia Kimberly
Born: Halloween, 2012
Hamilton, Ontario, Canada
To John and Kimberly – PROUD PARENTS!

When I was asked to participate in the Down Syndrome Diary, I was absolutely thrilled that our story could be included. You see, it is quite different from the previous authors, and has a really unique perspective. I hope that what I have to say can help readers to understand that a Down syndrome diagnosis is not a bad thing; that, after some initial discovery, it will be the most wonderful experience.

Before we get into my experience with Mia, I need to take you back over ten years. I was fortunate enough to meet and become very good friends with a lady approximately twenty years my senior, who had an amazing son who happened to have Down syndrome. At the time, he was in high school and he was quite involved in events through the Special Olympics.

He was a figure skater and a ten-pin bowler in organized teams by Special Olympics. It was a great pleasure to me to be able to accompany him to his practices and team tournaments, and to see the other participants with disabilities ranging from autism to prosthetic limbs, as well as Down syndrome.

We spent fun times together going to water parks and wrestling events (his absolute favourite!!). It was a lot of fun for me. I chose to return to college to become an Educational Assistant (I believe referred to as paras in the US). I trained for three years in school and was even assigned Down syndrome for my final project, randomly.

I had worked for four years on the school board when we became pregnant with Mia. During those four years, I had the opportunity to work with several students from age five to twenty that had Down syndrome. I saw how much they could achieve: whether it was reading Harry

Potter, creating amazing works of art on canvas, joining and excelling on the wrestling team, or doing an incredible job learning basic math skills. Every child had his/her own reasons to be proud of an accomplishment and each one was a reason for celebration. I love my job!

Now, on to Mia…

We found out at the twenty week anatomical ultrasound that Mia would be born with a heart defect. After a fetal echocardiogram, it was determined to be an AVDS (Atrial Ventricular Septal Defect), which is quite common in babies born with Down syndrome. She would need surgery at four months to correct the four holes in her heart. WOW – that is difficult and scary to hear. We are fortunate to live within an hour's drive of Toronto's Hospital for Sick Children (aka SickKids), where she would have the surgery, and recover completely. We had elected not to have prenatal screening tests at thirteen weeks, so we didn't have a genetic diagnosis. It was our belief that the results wouldn't matter, so why test!? However, at this point, the doctors suggested that we go through an amniocentesis, so we could be fully aware of the baby's genetic diagnosis. We had been told that, in addition to Trisomy 21-Down syndrome, there were a few other possibilities based on her heart defect. These possibilities were more than likely to be very severe, with many complications. We just wanted to know so we were prepared. The five days between amnio and results were very emotional for our family. We spent a lot of time talking and crying; the fear of the unknown was daunting.

Due to my experience working with many students with Down syndrome, I knew that the abilities of each child made them such amazing kids. Waiting for my own baby's diagnosis was made easier by this knowledge and experience. I am very lucky.

Receiving that phone call with a T-21 diagnosis was not so much a celebration, but relief. We knew she (we found out gender at this time as well) would have developmental and physical challenges, but we could prepare for and be strong for her.

We got involved with our local Down Syndrome Association and were able to speak with other parents who have gone down the same path of diag-

nosis prenatally. I cannot recommend this enough. Having other families to help you when you get this news is very comforting. Our association has a parent liaison who arranged get-togethers, and the association as a whole has events, parties, conferences, and "The Walk For Down Syndrome." It is a great community to be involved in. Seeing kids from birth to early adulthood, all with a common bond, is truly enlightening and an experience not to be missed.

Mia's birth was the best day of my life. She was this perfect (albeit blue) creature that loved me as much as I loved her. She was/is gorgeous and I am so very proud to be her mom!!!!

She had surgery to repair her heart at four and a half months old and came through it like a little trooper. She is so very strong, and has made us so happy with her tenacity and fighting spirit.

Now at age two and a half, she is showing us her abilities with building blocks and playing ball. She loves to read books and she enjoys her iPad as well as musical instruments.

She is learning the skills necessary to walk, but isn't quite there yet. She is, however, a great climber!

Age 2 - full of Personality!

To say that she gives us so much enjoyment is an understatement. We wouldn't trade her for anything!

Many hugs to you and your family,

Kimberly

P.S. We have just had word that Mia has been selected one of eight special needs children to attend a special preschool for 'our kids.' We cried like babies when we got the call; it was as if she had gotten into Harvard.

I love these moments and look forward to many, many more!

Hugs,

Kimberly

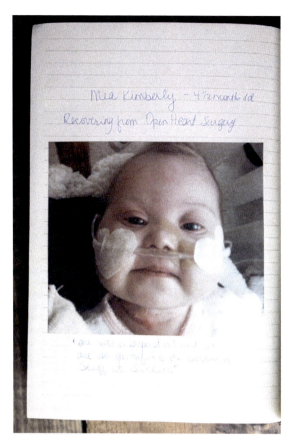

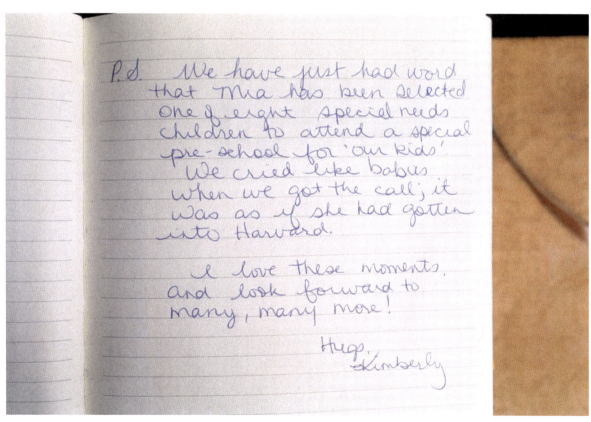

Mother's Day 2014

2021 Update:

Mia is now eight years old. She is a happy, well-rounded, kind, compassionate little girl. She is doing extremely well in school, reading just below her grade level. She enjoys speaking with her friends and family on video chats, asking everyone her favourite question, "What did you eat for breakfast?" For fun, Mia takes dance lessons and is on a Special Abilities cheerleading team, where she is the top of every pyramid! She is always jumping around and dancing, singing at the top of her lungs. This girl is destined to be a performer.

Everyone in our family is so proud of her and all she has accomplished. I've been told many times by family and friends how lucky they feel to have Mia in their lives. I must say, I agree!

Crystal & Lily

"It's okay that this is not what we had planned. It's okay that things don't always 'get better.' You just take a breath, close your eyes and start again."

—Crystal Trumper

Lillian Natalia
Born: December 2010
Toronto, Ontario, Canada

If four years ago you had told me that I would spend tonight watching our daughter, Lily, participate in her first school Spring concert, I'm not sure I would have believed you. If I'm being perfectly honest, I'm still not convinced it wasn't a dream. But photos and videos don't lie and the tears running down my face are proof that anything is possible.

If this life has taught me anything it's this lesson: life will never turn out the way you plan. Even when you think you have it all worked out, something will happen – a twist of fate, a stumble or fall or even a miracle – and you will find yourself at the beginning again. The biggest lesson in all of this is this – "And that's okay." (triple underline, exclamation point).

We thought that we had it all worked out. Lily's diagnosis did not come as a surprise to us – it was what brought her to us. My wife, Jessica, and I had always known that we would build our family through adoption and when we were asked if we would consider a child with special needs and Down syndrome in particular, we eagerly replied yes. We both have a background in working with children and adults with special needs and we knew what kind of joy it would bring to our lives. When our adoption worker showed us Lily's file, we fell head over heels in love and the three months it took for us to be "chosen" were the longest of our lives. When we finally got to bring her home, at five months old, we were over the moon.

Because we "knew" about Down syndrome (and I use quotations as I've learned that you can't really "know" until you've lived it). There was nothing in LIly's file that shocked or surprised us enough to "scare us off."

53

She had been diagnosed with a congenital heart defect, an AVSD, that is very common in children with Down syndrome. She had her first heart surgery at five days old and was scheduled for her second at six months. She was fed through an NG (naso-gastric) tube and was on two medications for reflux, but the expectations were that all of that would change once her heart was repaired. All of her therapists and her foster mother were pleased with her development – she made great eye contact, was curious, was making noises, and was getting stronger; she was exactly where we all wanted her to be. Jessica and I talked constantly about how she was going to walk and talk and be in an integrated class and how she was going to break down all of the stereotypes. We were so happy and confident. While we tried to empathize with other parents when they would discuss loss and grief, we felt like we knew a secret that they didn't yet – that this is a good life.

And then our world shifted. During Lily's second heart surgery, she was diagnosed with a condition called Pulmonary Vein Stenosis (PVS). I'll save you the medical textbook explanation, but generally the veins that bring oxygen-rich blood from the lungs to the heart get progressively more narrow until the blood supply is cut off completely. In Lily, the veins from her left lung are totally closed so her right lung has to do all of the work, which puts a lot of pressure on that lung and her heart.

Lily's surgeon attempted to repair it but told us there was nothing more, surgically, he could do for her. It felt like the bottom had fallen out beneath us.

Lily's recovery was long and filled with complications. We learned about PVS and it's a "wait and grow" disease. No one could tell us how long she would stay stable and we just had to wait and see how her body reacted as she grew. We looked PVS up on the internet and cried as we read words like, "heart-lung transplant" and "typically fatal." Finally, a month after her surgery, she was released and above everything else, we were just happy to be at home.

Five days. That's all the happiness we got.

On the morning of our fifth day at home, Lily went into a sudden cardiac arrest in Jessica's arms. We stood by, helpless, as paramedics and then the E.R. staff worked to bring her back to us. Thanks to them, she was revived and transferred back to the Hospital for Sick Children.

Gone were the days of trying to empathize with fear and loss – we were now thrown head first into it. As a result of the cardiac arrest, Lily suffered a significant brain injury that caused seizures, blindness, and massive developmental delays. Lily stopped moving, she stopped babbling and, the hardest for us, she stopped looking at us. In that single day, we felt as though all of our hopes and dreams were stolen away. We were facing a life that we weren't prepared for. We had to start again.

And that's okay!

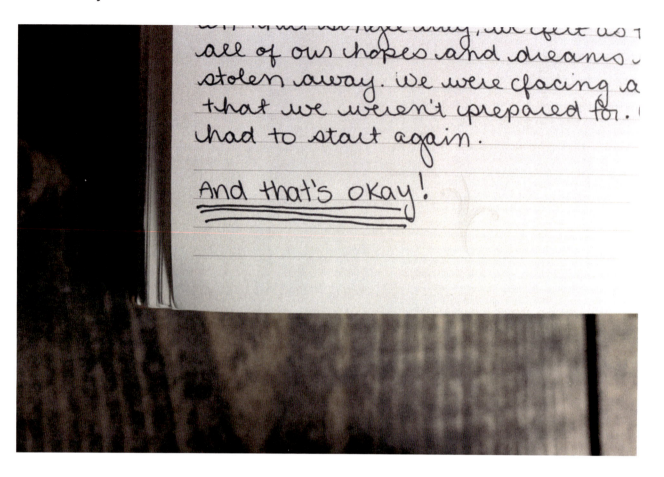

There it is – the lesson. It didn't happen overnight and it came with fears and frustrations and guilt, but we started to see it. This was an entirely new road, but it was okay. It started by taking joy in the smaller moments; the day that Lily held a string of bells and shook them ended with a dance party! We coined the term "Lily Time" and we live by that mantra; Lily will do everything in Lily-Time. She will do everything when she is ready and no amount of pushing, crying or pleading is going to change that. And that's okay!

It's okay that this is not what we had planned. It's okay that things don't always "get better." You just take a breath, close your eyes and start again.

Lily is now four years old and she is amazing (triple underline, exclamation point). Her heart and lungs are still stable and she has surpassed every medical expectation anyone had of her. She is on the verge of standing independently and is a breath away from saying her first word. She is almost at the end of her first year of Kindergarten and while she is in a special needs classroom, it's in an integrated school down the street and so she is part of her community. She laughs all of the time, even when she is the only one who knows what is funny.

~ Girl meets world
"Team Lily" - Sept. 2012 as adoption is finalized! ~

And tonight she was in her first school concert. She didn't sing along but she bounced and laughed and surprised us by sitting in her chair with total confidence.

It was what we expected, it wasn't what we planned and that's okay. To be honest, it may even be better – it's happiness in the most unexpected place.

With so much love,
Crystal

It wasn't what we expected, it wasn't what we planned and that's okay. To be honest, it may even be better - it's happiness in the most unexpected place.

with so much love,
Crystal ♡♡♡

Sweet ❀ child ✿

Holly & Jax

"If heart surgery is in your future let me tell you one thing.
You WILL get through it! I did and so will you. Our kids are
strong. They are fighters. They are determined."

—Holly Graham

Holly Graham
Medicine Hat, Alberta
June 2015

Jaxson James Graham
Born: April 24, 2014
Calgary, Alberta

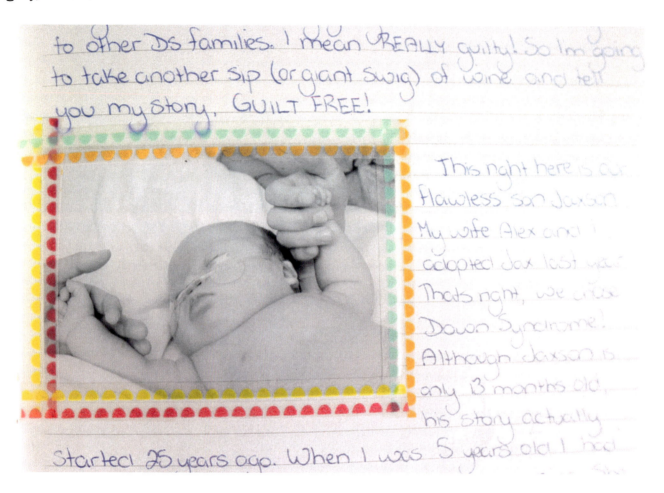

I can't believe that tonight I am sitting here with a glass of red wind in hand, finally writing in the Down Syndrome Diary! I have been sitting here for the last little while struggling to think of how I'm going to start my story. I'm going to be completely honest and tell you that I feel really guilty when I tell our story to other DS families. I mean REALLY guilty! So I'm going to take another sip (or giant swig) of wine and tell you my story. GUILT FREE!

This right here is our flawless son Jaxson. My wife Alex and I adopted Jax last year. That's right, we chose Down syndrome! Although Jaxson is only 13 months old, his story actually started 25 years ago. When I was 5 years old, I had a best friend named Mandy. Mandy was amazing. She was fun, happy, loving and had something magical about her. Mandy also had Down syndrome. I always knew Mandy was different from me. I didn't really know why, and it didn't matter.

Mandy left a HUGE imprint on my life. A few years after our friendship began, we moved houses and moved away from Mandy and her family. Around the age of 7, I came home from school one day and informed my mom that I was going to be a mommy to a baby just like Mandy one day…

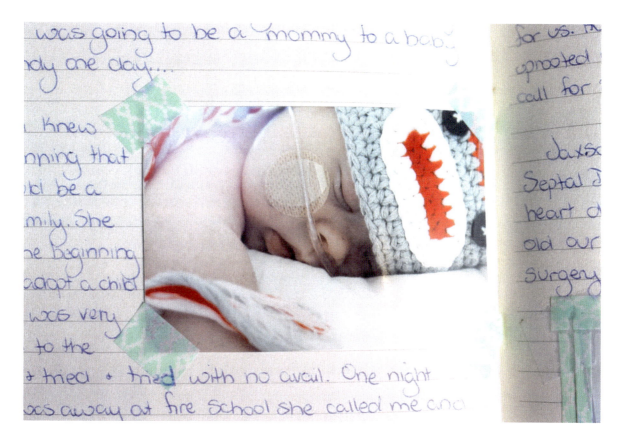

Alex and I knew from the beginning that adoption would be a part of our family. She knew from the beginning my desire to adopt a child with DS and was very much opposed to the idea. I tried and tried and tried to no avail. One night while Alex was away at fire school, she called me and said, "Ok, let's do this. Let's adopt a baby with Down syndrome." She had an "ah-ha" moment and within one week of her being home, we were filling out paperwork!

Fully expecting a long wait to be matched with a baby, we continued on with life. Four months after starting the adoption process, we got "the call" while on vacation in Las Vegas. We hopped on the next plane home, and 48 hours later we were holding our perfect son.

We were literally thrown into the world of parenting and Down syndrome.

Our bond to Jaxson was instant. He was meant for us, and we were meant for him. We quickly settled into our new life as parents. Jaxson was a very easy, content baby and made our transition to parenthood very smooth. However, it wasn't long before our lives were uprooted once again when we got the dreaded phone call for surgery.

Jaxson was born with AVSD (Atrioventricular Septal Defect) which is a very common congenital heart defect among babies with DS. At 11 weeks old our teeny tiny Jaxson went in for open heart surgery.

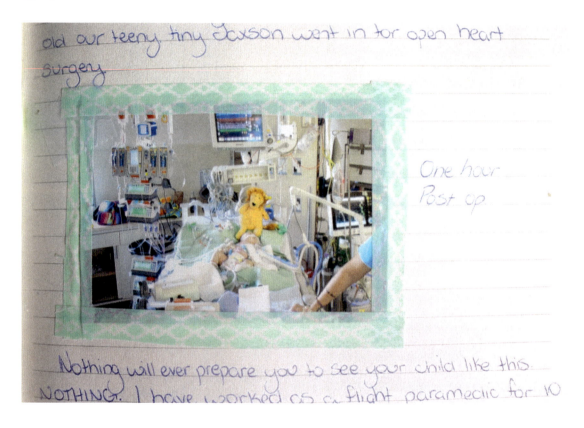

old our teeny tiny Jaxson went in for open heart surgery

One hour Post op

Nothing will ever prepare you to see your child like this. NOTHING. I have worked as a flight paramedic for 10

Nothing will ever prepare you to see your child like this. NOTHING. I have worked as a flight paramedic for 10 years. IV lines, ET tubes, chest tubes, ventilators, central lines, sick people, sick babies...I'm used to that! It's my job. It's what I do! Well, I don't "do" it when it's my son. Open heart surgery is downright terrifying. For some of you this may be in your future and for others it's an all too familiar sight. If heart surgery is in your future let me tell you one thing. You WILL get through it! I did and so will you. Our kids are strong. They are fighters. They are determined.

I am happy to report that today Jaxson's heart is A-OK! Jaxson had a few more health issues his first year (Bronchitis and RSV) but pulled through each illness like a champ. I'm sure if he could, he would tell his paranoid, hypochondriac mom (me) to calm down and quit worrying!

We just celebrated our first "Gotcha Day." One year of being a family! Let me tell you it has been one amazing year. Jaxson has grown like a weed on steroids. No one can believe it when we tell them our 21 lb. 13 month old tank was born with failure to thrive, was in heart failure, and needed open heart surgery. It has been such an honor to watch him grow and learn. He is a very smart boy who picks up on the smallest things.

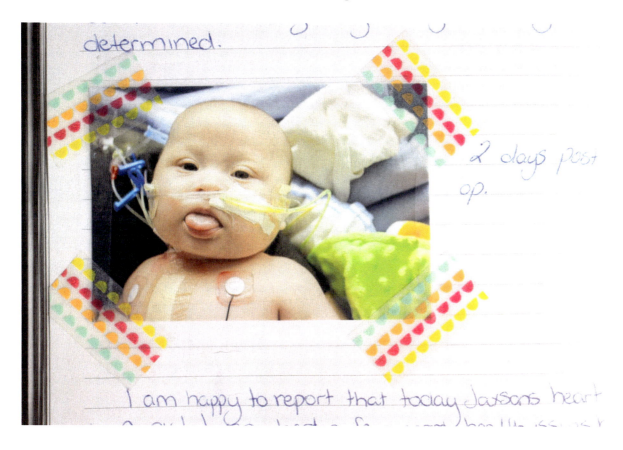

determined.

2 days post op.

I am happy to report that today Jaxsons heart

As expected, Jaxson is lagging behind the "typical" babies. At 13 months old, he isn't crawling, let alone walking. It's sad to watch his frustrations as he watches the other kids zooming around him as he's left stationary on the ground. Don't feel bad for him though. Jaxson works VERY hard in therapy, and he will get there. In the meantime we stay patient, and I will definitely enjoy having my baby for a wee bit longer than everyone else.

Perhaps my absolute favorite feature of Jaxson is his love for love. He is always hugging, snugging, pulling us in for sloppy open mouth baby kisses, and gently touching our faces. I've recently heard the story of a young lady with DS whose grandpa calls her 47th chromosome her "Love Chromosome." I am 100% sold on the fact that Jaxson also got the love chromosome .

At this point in my story, you're probably wondering why I feel guilty. I have talked to many DS moms who have shared with me their feeling of guilt and shame when they received the DS

time we stay patient and

ing my baby for a wee bit

on

eriously

g us

baby

hing

ara the

with Ds

47th

%.

axson

osome ♡

At this point in my story you're probably wondering why I feel guilty. I have talked to many Ds moms who have told me their feeling of guilt and shame when the got the Ds diagnosis. They suffered a loss and the death of the child they will never have. My personal guilt comes from our Ds journey being the complete opposite. Our journey has been so insanely positive, loving, happy and joyful. I can't relate, I can't empathize but I can completely understand.

The way I look at it is we just knew the secret before most others. The secret of how truly awesome and amazing Down syndrome is!

My biggest piece of advice I can leave you with is be patient! Smother your cutie with lots of love. Give them the tools they need with therapy. Then calm down relax and your child will do things when they are ready!

diagnosis. They suffered the loss and death of the child they will never experience. My personal guilt comes from our DS journey being the complete opposite from other family's experiences. Our journey has been so insanely positive, loving, happy, and joyful. I can't relate. I can't empathize but I can completely understand.

The way I look at it is we just know the secret before most others. The secret of how truly awesome and amazing Down syndrome is! I look at it like this – we just knew the secret before most others. The secret is that Down syndrome is truly awesome and amazing!

My biggest piece of advice I can leave you with is be patient! Smother your cutie with lots of love. Give them the tools they need with therapy. Then calm down, relax, and your child will do things when they are ready!

Jaxson's daily affirmation:

> You are smart and handsome,
> You are strong and brave,
> You are kind and special,
> You are loved Jaxson James.

With Lots of Love,
Holly, Alex, and Jaxson ❤️

Jaxsons daily affirmation:

You are smart and handsome,
You are strong and brave,
You are kind and special,
You are loved Jaxson James.

With lots of love,
Holly, Alex
and Jaxson

Mallory & Taitym

"This is the most beautiful journey that I never knew I wanted."

—Mallory Shuck

Mallory Shuck
Rothsay, Minnesota, USA
June 26, 2015

Taitym Olivea
5 30 2012

C can't believe it's finally my turn to write in the diary! I've had it for a few days and have been trying to find the perfect way to start Taitym's story.

Taitym was born May 30th, 2012. She was not diagnosed until she was around 3 months old. Her regular doctor heard a heart murmur and sent us to a specialist. We then had an echo and from that moment our lives were forever changed. The doctor called me into his office where I heard nothing that he said other than he was certain my sweet baby girl had Down syndrome. She also had a heart condition called Complete AV Canal Defect and was going to need open heart surgery as soon as she hit ten pounds.

I was in complete shock! From there we had a blood test to confirm – I was in complete denial. There was no way my perfect girl had Down syndrome! What were people going to say? Would they love her any less? I had so many fears for what was in store for Taitym.

The tests came back and confirmed my sweet baby had Down syndrome. The next few days are all a blur. We told very few people to begin with. I don't know why, but I didn't feel anyone needed to know as it shouldn't change how they felt about her.

At 6 months old, Taitym finally hit 10 pounds which meant it was time for open heart surgery. We met with the surgeon the day before surgery to go over details. The next morning was the scariest day of my life! Handing Taitym over to the nurses was almost impossible. I managed to do so and four hours later surgery was over and was a complete success (thank the Lord!). We were in the hospital for 5 days and then were discharged. Taitym rocked surgery and recovered great.

From then on, Taitym has been a healthy little girl with the exception of getting tubes placed in her ears.

Our lives are filled with many appointments and therapy sessions, but seeing her hit a milestone makes it all worth it.

Taitym became a big sister to Dalton on September 27, 2013. He is her biggest fan. He goes to all her appointments and does it with a smile. Dalton makes Taitym laugh harder than anyone else can!

"Every little boy is a super hero"

There are many days that are hard, and I wonder to myself if we can do this and then I look at Taitym, and I know anything is possible. This little girl can put a smile on anybody's face in 30 seconds!

Taitym has brought some of the greatest people into our lives! From local families all the way to people across the world. We have joined many groups and Facebook pages. You wouldn't believe how much you can become family to a person that you have never met! We cherish the bonds we have made with everyone. Taitym has many friends, some with Down Syndrome and some without, and even has her prom date already 😀.

are hard and I wonder to myself if we can do this and then I look at Taitum and I know anything is possible. This little girl can put a smile on anybodys face in 30 seconds!

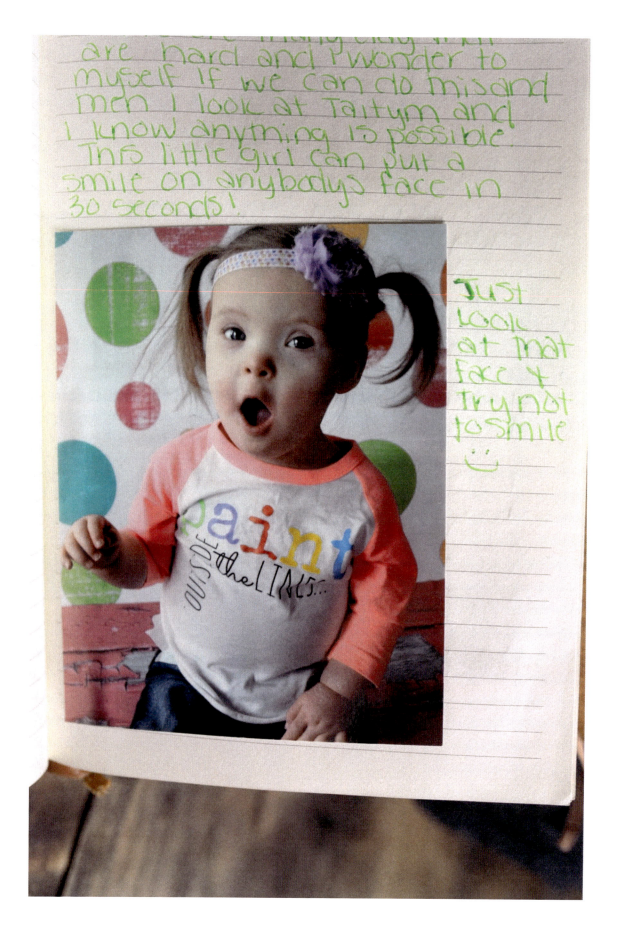

Just look at that face & Try not to smile :)

This is the most beautiful journey that I never knew I wanted. I wouldn't change anything about our journey. I can't wait to see what the future holds for Taitym. She's only three-years-old and is amazing!

My advice to a family new on this amazing journey is to embrace it!

"The difference between ordinary and extraordinary is just that little extra."

So welcome to the club!

With Lots of Love,
Mallory, Michael, Taitym, and Dalton

2021 Update:

Taitym is almost 9 and in 2nd grade. Big sister to Dalton, Berkley, Sutherlyn & Briggs. We moved to Fergus Falls and Taitym transferred schools where she has truly blossomed and has come so far in social skills, speech and more! We couldn't be more proud of the young lady she's becoming.

my advice to a family new
on this amazing journey
is to embrace it.

"The difference between
ordinary and extraordinary
is just that little extra"

So welcome to the club!

with lots of love,
Mallory, Michael,
Taitym & Dalton

Crystal & Brinkley

"The progress has been slow or at times, non-existent, but every moment is worth it. Every milestone is a victory. Every victory is a celebration."

—Crystal Holder

Brinkley
Crystal Holder
Williamston, SC, USA

August 2015

About ten years ago my husband Bryan and I started volunteering with an organization called Street Reach, which is sponsored by Brinkley Heights Ministries. They are based in Memphis, TN, and provide programs aimed at keeping inner-city street youths off the streets. The goal of Street Ranch is to break the cycle of drugs and gangs by preparing those involved in their programs to "take back" their neighborhood and city.

The families at Brinkley Heights fight and advocate everyday for the children in their community. They have a faith like no other. They truly believe that our God is faithful and will answer their prayers to take back their community. Their faith and perseverance have left a huge impression on us.

Our experience with the children in the Brinkley Heights community helped us decide to become foster parents. In December of 2008, after seven years of marriage, we welcomed our first foster child into our home. He was a beautiful little six month old baby boy named Reese. Although the process was long and drawn out, we finally adopted Reese in September of 2011. We soon realized that our family was not complete so we started trying to get pregnant.

Although we got pregnant after a few years of trying, we lost the baby early on in the pregnancy. After some soul searching and a lot of prayer, we decided to try again. In early 2012, we were once again successful, but similar to my first pregnancy, I was incredibly sick the entire time. Given my history, my doctor was overly cautious and watched me very closely.

At our twenty week ultrasound, we were excited to learn that we were having a baby boy. However, during the exam I could tell something wasn't right, but the technician didn't say anything. Having already suffered a miscarriage, I felt incredibly uneasy. A short time later, my doctor met with us to explain the results. There were concerns about his heart and about him having a fold on his neck. She wanted to refer us to a specialist and suggested that I complete some of the testing I had opted out of earlier on in the pregnancy. We agreed to both and waited to see what would happen.

A few days later, the doctor called to discuss the results of my blood work. She informed us that the risk for our baby being born with Down syndrome was quite high (1 in 4). She assured me that she would support us every step of the way and connect us with all the resources we would need. More importantly, she never entertained any thoughts other than us raising our child to be the best he could be.

Following our initial visit with the high-risk specialist and genetic counselor, we received the results from our amniocentesis. The results confirmed the diagnosis and we began our journey with Down syndrome. Our next visit to the specialist included a consultation with a pediatric cardiologist for a more thorough examination of our baby's heart. After completing a fetal echocardiogram, we met with the cardiologist who delivered yet another diagnosis. Our son would be born with Tetralogy of Fallot. This diagnosis came with a set of worries all of its own, which was all very overwhelming. I think the cardiologist could sense how we were feeling and asked if he could pray for us. We gladly took him up on the offer and he prayed for us right there and then.

It felt as though so many things were "coming at me" and I soon realized that what I really needed was wisdom – the wisdom to build a team of professionals around us, to know how to explain things to our family (especially Reese) and to locate the necessary resources while deciphering what was good information versus what to ignore.

We also knew that our sweet baby boy would need to be strong, determined, and a fighter. He would also need a strong faith. Knowing the struggles our sweet baby would face, we knew the name Brinkley would be a perfect fit for him. Our family at Brinkley Heights epitomized all of these things.

As my pregnancy progressed, I experienced some complications which were in turn putting Brinkley at risk. At thirty-four weeks, our care team decided that it was no longer safe to prolong the pregnancy. Brinkley was delivered by emergency C-section on September 6, 2012. He was born six weeks premature, weighing 3 pounds, 2.2 ounces, and 17 inches long. He spent his first seven weeks in the NICU where his biggest struggle was learning to eat. It is not uncommon for babies with Down syndrome to have this problem due to their hypotonia (low

tone). At five weeks old, a G-tube was placed which helped with his feeding and got us one step closer to going home.

Given Brinkley's heart issues, we knew he would need open heart surgery at some point. He was twelve weeks old when he was readmitted for his first open heart surgery, after only being home from the NICU for five weeks. Unfortunately, his recovery was quite difficult, and he remained in hospital for another five weeks, which forced us to spend his first Christmas and New Year's in the hospital. We returned home only to be surprised six weeks later with an unexpected hospital admission. Brinkley received his "helper heart" (a pacemaker) on February 14, 2013. Thankfully, the admission was short and life got back to normal fairly quickly.

Aside from Brinkley having heart problems, he also had on-going respiratory issues that went undiagnosed for months. Luckily, our prayers for wisdom were answered and the Lord placed a third year resident on Brinkley's medical team. This young doctor was determined to help him and to get us the answers we needed – and he did just that! Although it took a few months and some referrals, a scope of Brinkley's airway and a forty-five minute procedure solved our respiratory issues.

surprise is what a blessing they are and how much they enrich the lives of everyone around them.

I could go on and on, but I'll just say Congratulations! The best is yet to come!

You can follow us at:
www.themommyonamission.blogspot.com

Instagram: @holdercd or @brinkleyrocks

Facebook: Team Brinkley

Although our first twelve to eighteen months were difficult, it was all worth it. Brinkley is now a few days shy of his third birthday and he is absolutely perfect! We see many doctors and keep a full therapy schedule. The progress has been slow, or at times non-existent, but every moment is worth it. Every milestone is a victory. Every victory is a celebration. And celebrating is what Brinkley does best.

Our most recent celebration has been for learning to walk. It took nearly three full years, but as of July we have a walker. He does everything that he wants to, in his time. It may seem like it will never happen, but just wait. These kids are full of surprises. I think the biggest surprise is what a blessing they are and how much they enrich the lives of everyone around them. I could go on and on, but I'll just say congratulations! The best is yet to come.

You can follow us at www.themommyonamission.blogspot.com.
Instagram: @holdercd or @brinkleyrocks
Facebook: Team Brinkley

Angela & Sam

"My husband proudly announced, 'It's a boy!' and my heart was overjoyed. Then I realized how quiet the room was."

—Angela Olsen

Angela Olsen – Written 2015

Samuel Thomas Amani Olsen
Born May 24, 2012
Duluth, Minnesota

Meaning of Amani: Peace (Swahili)

Early Signs

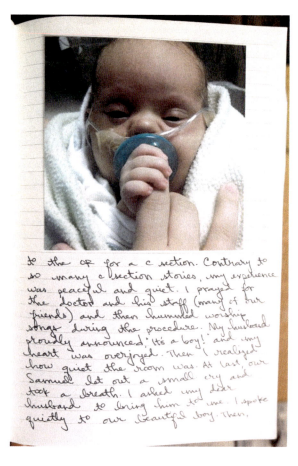

to the OR for a c section. Contrary to so many c section stories, my experience was peaceful and quiet. I prayed for the doctor and his staff (many of our friends) and then hummed worship songs during the procedure. My husband proudly announced "It's a boy!" and my heart was overjoyed. Then I realized how quiet the room was. At last, our Samuel let out a small cry and took a breath. I asked my dear husband to bring him to me. I spoke quietly to our beautiful boy. Then,

The first whisper of Down syndrome in our family was when I was pregnant with my sweet Samuel, just after our twenty week lab work. I received a phone call from our family doctor, a dear friend of ours, saying there was a chance our baby had Down syndrome. She said she wanted a specialist to do a level two ultrasound for a closer look. I was surprised, but I also remembered reading it isn't all that uncommon to get a positive result and then not actually have an extra chromosome. I told my husband, we prayed together, and then we waited for the nurse to call. When she called, she was rushed and very matter-of-fact. As soon as I hung up, I cried. I was scared for my baby and for our future, but I knew, deep in my heart, that his diagnosis wouldn't change the love we had for our baby. We went in the next day, answered a list of questions with a genetic counselor, and sat through a very in-depth ultrasound that showed nothing but a healthy baby. Not a single soft marker. We were encouraged. We declined the offer to do an amnio, feeling peace through the remainder of the pregnancy. To avoid unnecessary worry, my husband and I chose not to tell anyone about the possibility of Down syndrome, though we did a little reading to prepare ourselves, just in case. We prayed over our baby and, by the grace of God, we truly forgot about the possibility of Down syndrome through my third trimester.

Birth

The afternoon of May 23, 2012, I found myself in labor. It was two weeks before my due date, so I was a little surprised, as my daughter had been eight days late. My husband came home to check my progress (one of the perks of being married to a doctor) and verified the baby was on the way! By the time we got to the hospital, I was at 8cm. I progressed so quickly, I wasn't able to get an epidural. I had been pushing for three hours when the doctors informed me the baby was beginning to show signs of distress. I was wheeled to the OR for a C-section. Contrary to so many C-section stories, my experience was peaceful and quiet. I prayed for the doctor and his staff (many of our friends) and then hummed worship songs during the procedure. My husband proudly announced, "It's a boy!" and my heart was overjoyed. Then I realized how quiet the room was. At last, our Samuel let out a small cry and took a breath. As my husband held him, I spoke softly to our baby boy, and he opened his eyes for his first glimpse of me. As our eyes met, I knew. I knew that my sweet baby, with his beautifully almond-shaped eyes, had Down syndrome. I didn't need a test to confirm it. My mama instinct just knew. And I felt peace.

when I would look at my boy and not have my first thought be of Down syndrome. It took a year, maybe, but I now see Samuel and all of his personality and potential long before I see his diagnosis. He is amazing!

KENYA
I have always had a great desire to live and teach in a developing country. When I met my husband at the end of college, we knew he would go through medical school, we would start our family, and then we would move

Early Days

We learned very early that there are many emotions tied to being the parents of a child with Down syndrome. My husband went through a mourning process while Sam was still in the NICU. This was not the son he had imagined. He loved Sam fiercely from day one, but it was going to take time to get used to the changed expectations. I, however, didn't mourn until Sam came home. In our quiet moments together, I would look into Sam's eyes and feel tremendous guilt, as though his diagnosis was my fault. I felt I had failed him as a mother. In my head, I knew it wasn't true, but it took a little longer for my heart to believe it. I wondered if there would ever be a time when I would look at my boy and not have my first thoughts be of Down syndrome. It took a year maybe, but I now see Samuel and all of his personality and potential long before I see his diagnosis. He is amazing!

Kenya

I have always had a great desire to live and teach in a developing country. When I met my husband at the end of college, we knew he would go through medical school, we would start our family, and then we would move to East Africa. We were setting up our first trip to Kenya when Sam was born. We had been expecting a healthy, typically-developing baby and had never imagined otherwise, so for the slightest moment, we were unsure of what his diagnosis meant for the future of our family. As we prayed about it the night he was born, we felt great peace that Sam's extra chromosome was a surprise to us, but it wasn't to God. We still felt called to East Africa, so when Sam was seven months old, we packed our bags and hopped on a plane. Twenty-four hours later, we landed in Kenya where we lived near a rural hospital for two months. We learned what life might be like for us with homeschooling, learning Swahili, and living amongst the Kenyan people. And we went on Safari! (During which Sam mostly slept.) We fell in love. Yes, we will have to work hard to ensure Sam gets therapies and all the education he needs, but I have a Master of Education and we will always live near a hospital, so resources will be available.

One thing we discovered in Kenya was the extreme lack of resources and education for children with special needs. That is something we are passionate about changing. We will be moving to Kenya long-term in the Summer of 2016, and we want to make it a high priority to connect families with resources and to train teachers how to work with varying abilities in their village classrooms. We would not have been aware of the intense need for this without our Samuel. We truly believe Sam's determination and joy is going to impact people who haven't yet had the opportunity to see the incredible potential of someone with special needs.

THOUGHTS TO NEW PARENTS

- Don't forget to be kind to yourself. Parenting is a learning process in any situation, so allow extra space for emotions, changed expectations, and new experiences as you parent your child with Down syndrome.
- Any emotions you have after learning your child has Down syndrome are okay. Feeling angry or frustrated or hurt doesn't make you a bad parent. It's okay and healthy to grieve.
- Surround yourself with positive support. This makes a world of difference. If you can't find anyone in your area, there are countless parent networks on Facebook and Instagram. Ask questions and celebrate milestones together!
- Keep dreaming! Life doesn't need to come to a halt because your child has Down syndrome. The pace of life may change, but there are still so many possibilities.

Sending love from our family to yours.

THE OLSENS

Pete, Angela, Ella & Sam

2021 Update: Sam is now nearly nine years old and is in 2nd grade. We did move to Kenya when Sam was five. He loved making new friends around the hospital, going on safari drives, and playing outside every day. After 13 months in Africa, we made the hard decision to move back to Minnesota because Sam was really struggling with his speech development. He has since grown tremendously in every area. In August 2020, we moved to Florida where Sam is continuing to get amazing therapies, plays soccer on a local team, and loves being at the beach. He has the best imagination and is hilarious. We're so proud of who he is and everything he has done!

Sending love from our family to yours,

THE OLSENS
Pete, Angela, Ella & Sam

www.TheMangoMemoirs.com

♡

Meriah & Moxie

"After months of deep reflection, I came to a place in which I realized that although Moxie and I both have disabilities, her life is not mine. Her path is not mine. It is hers alone."

—Meriah Nichols

Meriah Nichols
Hawaii, USA
Written 2015

Dear You,

I t's weird to be holding a pen in my hand. Once an avid journaler, I swapped my pen and paper out for the computer and became an avid blogger instead. It works.

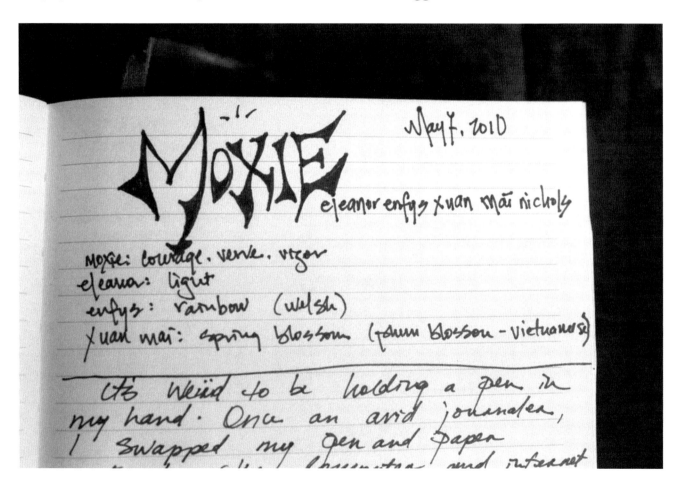

And it's weird to be talking about Moxie's birth and all of the early Down syndrome stuff again. I wrote so much the first few years that I don't think I have much else to say.

It's like a pentimento though – when a painting was painted upon an existing painting. Over time, the new painting fades and you can see traces of the original painting. So it is with Moxie's story, and the glimmers of my painting showing through hers.

You see, I am deaf, I have an auditory processing disorder, TBI and C-PTSD.

These are pieces of who I am and I struggled for years to heal and to develop pride in them, in myself. I had finally reached a place of personal peace and acceptance when my unborn daughter was diagnosed with Down syndrome via amniocentesis.

That diagnosis...just about knocked me over.

In that process of being knocked over and feeling my way back up again, a huge decision was made, which was the choice to *not* terminate her life, even when pressured to by my doctors. *You might be wondering why it was difficult for me to choose to keep her, right?* I mean, I had achieved some personal peace and acceptance regarding my own disabilities, after all.

But it was exactly that: I KNEW WHAT I WAS GETTING INTO.

I knew something of what my life as a parent of a child with Down syndrome would entail. I knew what pieces would be hard. I knew SO MUCH that no one else except another person with a disability could ever know.

It's like being white and choosing to adopt a black child. You "think" you know, but since you are white, you really don't.

I knew – from my own personal experience – about disability discrimination, about systemic prejudice. I knew about the horrific sexual abuse statistics, about all the barriers to education and employment. I knew about the SSI marriage penalties, about disability hierarchy, tokenism. I knew how it feels to have people look at you, mock you, look away, exclude you, reject you, use you.

Who could possibly want that for their child?

After months of deep reflection, I came to a place in which I realized that although Moxie and I both have disabilities, **her life is not mine**. Her path is not mine. It is hers alone. I can do my part to be aware, protect and guide her, push for change in our society, etc., but her path is hers. It will not necessarily be even a fraction as painful as mine was.

Ten years later and I see the truth in that piece. She is joyful, strong, confident. It's not to say that she doesn't have challenges; she does. She faces challenges in school and daily life as everyone does. The difference is that she has the self-assurance and skill sets to both protect and propel her.

In the Down syndrome community I hear a lot of parents talking about how their child with Down syndrome is their hero, an inspiration, or has changed their lives.

As I see it, what happens is that our child opens a portal to a world that gives us a broader and more visible opportunity to be – to grow into – our most authentic selves.

Our children do not *give* us courage; our children provide us with more opportunities to *develop* our courage, because we are placed in more situations in which we can make the choice to be courageous.

In this, it is always our choice to develop our courage, to continue to learn and to apply what we've learned.

Love,
Meriah

Unpacking Disability with Meriah Nichols – https://www.meriahnichols.com
FB: facebook.com/meriahnichols
Instagram: @unpackingdisability
Twitter: @meriahnichols

Karen & Liam

"I knew nothing about Down Syndrome. Did we want to bring a child into the world that may never have a normal life?"

—Karen Brady

Karen Brady
Orlando, Florida, USA

December 1, 2015

Liam Tyler Brady
D.O.B. 8/31/12

I 've been waiting for this Diary to reach me for a year, and now I would like to share my story.

It is very similar to everyone else's story, and I am going to be 100% honest.

Before I begin, let me first tell you my brief history. I have 3 daughters from a previous marriage, and when I re-married, we decided to try for a boy. It took a while, but I finally got pregnant. My husband was overjoyed. This was his first child. Things were going fine until my 17th week. We went in for an ultrasound and there was no heartbeat. We were beyond devastated. I chose to not have a DNC and decided to deliver the baby. There is no sadder feeling than to walk into the hospital maternity floor and have to explain to the nurse why you are there. To know that when it's all said and done, you will leave empty handed.

I delivered our baby boy later that night. Labor pains and all. We cried and decided we would not try for another baby. It was too much for us. It took a long time, but we healed, physically and emotionally.

About a year later, I talked my hubby into trying again. Our first baby died because it had Trisomy 18, and the doctor said we had a pretty good chance of having a normal child should we decide to try again.

We finally got pregnant after a long time of trying. During the previous pregnancy, I had opted out of any testing, but we chose to have them done this time. I was a little nervous, but not too worried. The doctor's office called to tell me that I needed to come in right away to discuss results. They said there was a chance the baby could have Down syndrome. If I wanted, I could have an amnio done and that would be more accurate. It's a dangerous procedure, but I had it done when I was pregnant with my twins so I knew what it entailed.

We waited 10 days for the results. When the doctor told us that our baby had Down syndrome, my husband and I both cried. Our doctor was kind and told us our options. I couldn't think straight. I couldn't remember anything we talked about after he told us. We went home to figure things out.

My husband was pretty set on not continuing with the pregnancy. I was torn. I knew nothing about Down syndrome. Did we want to bring a child into the world that may never have a normal life? What about my 3 girls? Would they be left to take care of a sick sibling when we were no longer around? I tried doing research, but it made me more depressed.

I didn't want to put my family through that, but I also don't believe in abortion. However, when you are put in the situation of having to make that decision, everything I stood for was unclear. I did worry that my husband would leave and not be able to handle a disabled child. We agreed to make an appointment at a clinic to terminate the pregnancy. I was sad. I could feel my baby move inside me, and I tried not to get attached. I read about what the procedure would entail. I did it mostly to keep my husband from being resentful, but I decided that I would wait for a sign from God regardless.

A week before I was scheduled for the procedure, they called to tell me they needed to cancel my appointment and I would have to reschedule. That was my sign, but my husband didn't see it that way. We had a long talk, and we both decided that we would have the baby. I felt such a relief, but I still worried about how he would treat the baby once he was born. I asked him if he would love him, and he said he didn't know.

The weeks went by, and he was very distant. He never talked about our baby, but he was supportive of me. There were a lot of arguments about his family bloodline dying out and how much harder this was for him because this would be his only child, and I already had 3 "normal" kids. It was a trying time.

Finally the day came to deliver our baby. We had to schedule the C-section 5 weeks premature because I had too much fluid build up. The drive to the hospital was so quiet. It felt like we were going to a funeral. He stayed with me until they took me away to prep for the surgery. At that point as I waited for him to come to the room, I broke down and cried like a baby. The nurses

P.S. As I read back on what I've written I just want to add that Liam Is growing up in a loving Family. He's so smart and I can't wait to see the wonderful things he will accomplish! Choosing to say yes to a life with him not only blessed my life but everyone else that is a part of our lives, not just today but for future generations! Liam, you will do great things!

asked if I was ok, and I told them I was worried because our baby has Down syndrome, and I didn't know how my husband would feel. All those months of being strong and brave just poured out of me.

After my husband was back with me, I delivered Liam. And suddenly I didn't care about his diagnosis anymore. All I wanted was my beautiful baby and to know that he was ok.

He spent a month in NICU. He was born with no anal opening so at 2 days old (and while I was at a different hospital), he had his first surgery to repair that. Then 3 days later, they did another surgery to attach a colostomy bag so his first surgery would heal properly. He was jaundiced and had breathing issues. He had a small opening in his heart and had a ton of doctors taking care of him. It was so overwhelming! They couldn't tell me when he would be able to come home, but it would be a while.

He was finally allowed to leave after learning to feed from a bottle properly. It was the best day ever! I finally had my little boy all to myself. No more nurses and machines and feeling like he belonged to the hospital.

We saw many doctors the first year. His cardiologist cleared him. The hole in his heart had closed up. We see an ENT doctor for his hearing. He has had 2 sets of tubes put in for fluid not draining. His colostomy was reversed when he was 5 months old. He went to a urologist for an enlarged kidney and bladder reflux which is all better now. He takes meds and sees an Endocrinologist for his hypothyroidism. He takes daily Miralax for constipation and sees a GI doctor for reflux and bowel issues.

Liam gets therapy 3 times a week for OT, PT, and speech. Life was very busy to say the least, but it's all been so he can have the best outcome possible.

He has finally learned how to walk even if it did take a bit longer than usual. He was about 2 ½. He never wanted to crawl so he got around by scooting on his butt for the longest time. I've come to realize that he will reach milestones when he's ready and not when I expect it. I also can't compare him to other kids because everyone learns at a different pace. That's not to say that I don't get sad or discouraged at times. Liam is not a good eater, and he is hard to feed. He is also not talking, so we both get frustrated when we can't figure out what he wants.

I won't lie and say that it's not hard, but no one ever said parenting would be easy no matter the child. Liam has brought so much joy into our family. He loves his sisters and daddy.

He's sweet, spirited and calm. He's taught us all to take life one day at a time and enjoy small accomplishments.

Even though it took my husband a little longer to come around, he did. He loves his little buddy and to hear him tell Liam that just melts my heart. There are times I still struggle with the DS and wish he didn't have this. It's not because I would love him any less, but because I never want him to be treated with unkindness or to be hurt by cruel words. It is because I don't want him to struggle with learning things. This is the blessing God gave to us, and I feel honored to be his mommy.

I don't know where this journey will take us, but now my purpose is to be an advocate for Liam. I'm currently trying to figure out a way to get the Catholic school my girls attend to allow Liam to go there. How is it possible to preach the love of God and then turn away our children with special needs? I want the best future possible for my son, and I'll move mountains if I have to!

So if you're reading this book, please know that we all understand how you may feel about a diagnosis. You may need time to process it all before you decide you want to talk to someone and that's ok. It's not the end of the world even though it may feel that way. You will mourn and be sad and angry and that's ok too. But know that there is a light at the end of the tunnel. When you're holding that baby, nothing will matter more than the love you have for that precious life in your arms. Enjoy those special moments because before you know it, they grow up and become independent individuals that will continue to bring love to the people they are surrounded by.

Please contact me if you need to talk.
    bradygirls4@gmail.com

Or on Instagram
    @liamrulestheworld

P.S. As I read back what I've written, I just want to add that Liam is growing up in a loving family. He is so smart, and I can't wait to see the wonderful things he will accomplish! Choosing to say 'yes' to a life with him not only blessed my life but everyone else that is part of our lives… And not just today, but for future generations! Liam, you will do great things!

So if you're reading this book, please know that we all understand how you may feel about a diagnosis. You may need time to process it all before you decide you want to talk to someone and that's ok. It's not the end of the world even though it may feel that way. You will mourn and be sad/angry and that's ok too. But know that there is a light at the end of the tunnel. When you're holding that baby nothing will matter more than the love you have for that precious life you hold. Enjoy those special moments because before you know it they grow up and become independant individuals that will continue to bring love to the people they are surrounded by.

Please contact me if you need to talk

bradygirls4@gmail.com

or on Instagram

@brady2girl

Patricia & Sara

"Out of my four children she's the only one who attended prom. The one thing I cried about for her, none of my other kids cared to do!"

—Tricia Goins

Tricia Goins & Sara
December 12, 2015
Nassau Bay, Texas
USA

"She will never walk, talk, read, or attend school – and by one year of age the back of her head will flatten."

I was only 22 years old when the doctor said these words to me just a few weeks after my first daughter Sara was born. I remember looking down at my baby who I had dressed to the nines to see the geneticist that day and thinking, "I'll show you."

I took Sara home and I loved her. We attended therapy three times a week, I taught her sign language; even though baby sign wasn't a popular thing in 1992! Everything became a learning experience; auditory, visual, tactile – stimulation was always the goal. Honestly, I was just winging it. There was so little real information available, and no Internet to do a Google search or connect with other parents. Anything she received was cobbled together or done by instinct.

The therapy and doctor appointments helped me as much as they helped Sara. It was a welcome distraction from all of the scary "what ifs" and unknowns of the future. I'm not going to lie – I was scared. The darkest points were ones where I would recite the laundry list of things Sara would never do; driving, a boyfriend, prom, living alone. I would sit and wonder what would happen if I died? Who would love and protect her?

That's the funny thing about fear and the unknown. You worry about so many things that never actually turn out to be, and then the things that happen that you never saw coming. I'm pretty sure that's the definition of parenting!

Right before Sara started high school I took her shopping. It was so important to me that she have the right clothes, haircut, and brand new Hollister bag because HIGH SCHOOL, gotta fit in and look the part, right?

That first day of school Sara walked into the kitchen looking like any other high school girl and said, "Mom can you tie my shoes?" As I knelt down to tie her brand new oh-so-perfect shoes I lost it. I was sending her off into a world of grown kids and she couldn't tie her own shoes. I took a breath and composed myself before I stood back up. Those mile marker moments are the hardest, the tiny tsunamis that hit you when you least expect it.

I'm so proud to say that Sara did grow up to walk, dance, talk, sing, read, write, have a boyfriend, and attend so many proms that we've lost count! All those things I was so scared she wouldn't do, she's done so much and left such a positive impact on anyone she meets. In 2013 she proudly crossed the stage and received her high school diploma.

Out of my four children she's the only one who attended prom. The one thing I cried about for her, none of my other kids cared to do!

Sara also has three younger siblings. Growing up with a sibling with Down syndrome gave my children a higher acceptance of others' differences. They see people first instead of disabilities. We made a point to never treat Sara as the center of our family. We treated her just like any of the other kids with the same expectations of being a good human.

Sara is 29 years old now and has a full and meaningful life. She goes out with friends, bowls, swims, and runs track for Special Olympics. She goes to Zumba class and attends a day program. Out of all of us, Sara's social calendar is always full.

Every year on Sara's birthday, I write a letter to the geneticist who told me all those years ago what my daughter would never do. Looking back on those letters I can see how far she's come and how much she's accomplished.

Sara & William have dated for 4 years now. They met in school, and she lovingly refers to him as her "hot tamale". They enjoy date nights, The Walking Dead, going to the Boardwalk and movies. To watch them together makes my heart happy.

Sara also has three younger siblings. Growing up with a sibling who has Down Syndrome gave my children a higher acceptance of others differences. They see people first - not disabilities.

If I could go back and tell my 22 year old self any one thing, it would be, "What feels like today to be such a tragedy will one day be your greatest triumph."

Also…

- Connect with other parents who have a child with Down syndrome
- Join/volunteer with Special Olympics
- When your child is school aged – join a Buddy Program (best buddies)
- Remember that YOU are your child's best advocate
- Never set a ceiling on what your child will learn or do
- Enjoy the achievements and celebrate the smallest accomplishments
- It's okay to be scared sometimes. Parenting <u>any</u> kid can be a scary thing!

Raising Sara has not made me special or somehow chosen. I did what any woman does when she becomes a mom; I loved her.

Sara did the rest!

You can follow me on Instagram at: @jewelboxhouse or email me at tandtgoins@gmail.com

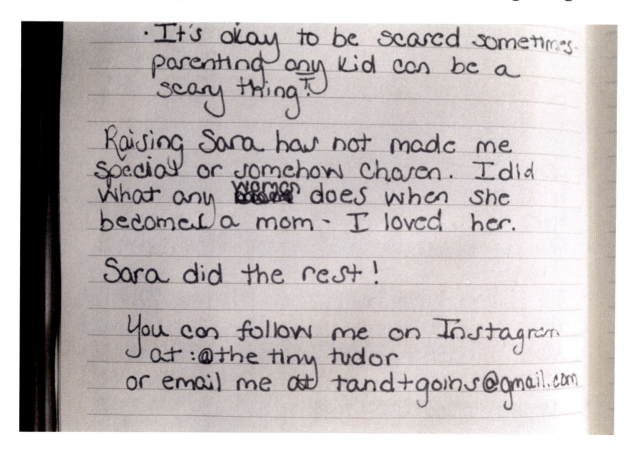

Sara's Entry:
Sara Keller
29 years old
Texas

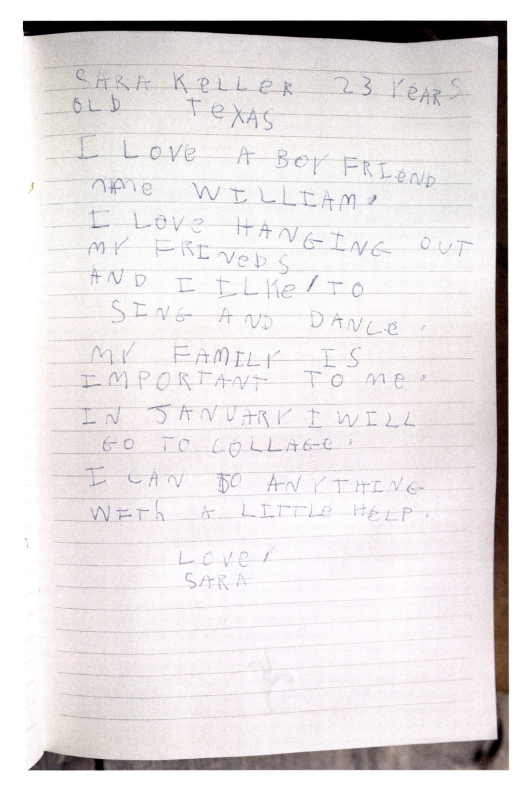

I love hanging out with my family and friends. I like to sing and dance. My family is important to me. I graduated from high school, attended junior college, and I go to a day program where I'm involved in lots of activities. I can do anything with a little help.

Love, Sara

I graduated from high school.

I can do anything!

Chelsey & Emersyn

"These fears are things I have really never chosen to talk about with anyone besides my husband, and now here I am opening my heart to anyone who wants to know – hoping it can help anyone who needs it."

—Chelsey Elder

Emersyn Beth Elder
October 27, 2013
Born in Oklahoma
Written by: Chelsey Elder AKA Mommy
On January 8, 2016

Emersyn
October 27, 2013 4:32 am

Little one, when you play,
Pay no heed what they say.
Let your eyes sparkle and shine,
Never a tear, baby of mine.
        "Baby Mine" from Dumbo

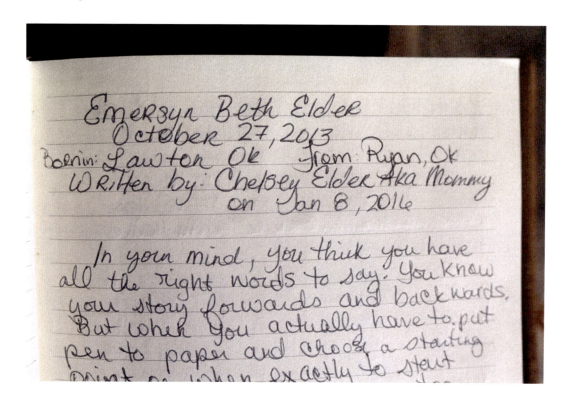

In your mind, you think you have all the right words to say. You know your story forwards and backwards. But when you actually have to put pen to paper and choose a starting point of when exactly to start telling it, the task becomes too challenging. I've been thinking about this precious diary for over a year now – and yet I feel unprepared. Similar to how I felt when we received a Down syndrome diagnosis – with all that in mind – I've decided to wing it – to keep it raw and just go with it.

Psalm 139 : 13-14
For you created my inmost being;
you knit me together in my mother's
womb. I praise you because I am
fearfully and wonderfully made;
your works are wonderful, I know
that full well.

The moment I found out I was pregnant, on my husband's birthday no less, I knew our whole world was about to change. Really, we had no idea just how much. I sometimes wish I could go back and do it all again with all the strength and confidence that motherhood has provided me, and other times I thank God that I never have to relive it again.

For me, pregnancy was no easy task. For the first 17 weeks, I was extremely sick with "all day" sickness. There were some days I was fully dependent on a pb&j sandwich for my caloric intake. It was also in week 17 that we started having ultrasounds every 2 weeks to measure my cervix. Lucky for us, we found out then we were having a girl! We hadn't decided on it previously, but sitting in the office that day we knew her name.

→ ❤️ Emersyn Beth ❤️ ←

For some women, they don't form a connection with their children until the day they are born or the following days after their birth. For me, it was this moment. Seeing her precious profile, her tiny hand, her cute little butt, love just came pouring into my heart!

Love! Love! Love! Love!

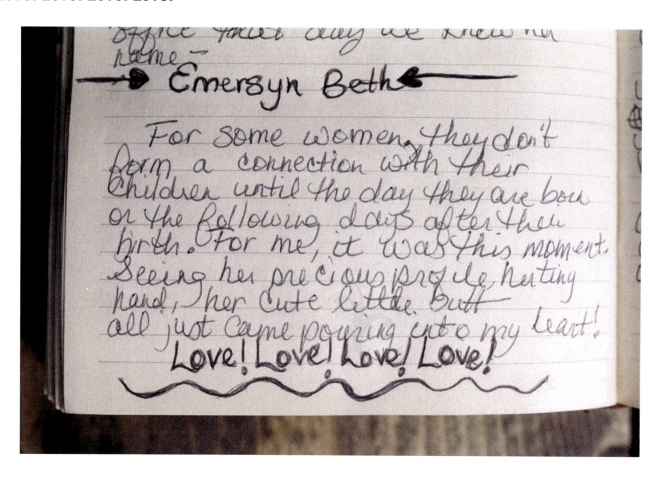

The reason for measuring my cervix is because I have a short one, which is scary stuff. Mine stayed at 2.5cm and they stopped monitoring around week 23, telling me to take it easy with the addition of a few restrictions.

We finally reached the 3rd trimester and that's when I was diagnosed with gestational diabetes. Each trimester had its own set of worries. This one was awful. Telling an already stressed pregnant woman that she can't have sweets is its own form of evil! I saw a dietitian every 2 weeks and had a non-stress test where they monitored Emersyn's activity.

Through all these worries, I managed to find a silver lining. I didn't gain as much weight and I frequently got to hear Emersyn's heartbeat.

At my week 35 appointment, I went into my first of the weekly appointments filled with joy that we were now in the home stretch! My doctor felt for Emersyn's size – she got an alarmed look on her face and told me Emersyn felt small. My mind started spinning – small? They had prepared me for a big baby! I went for an emergency ultrasound in the hospital. I remember looking at that screen and seeing her measuring at 33 weeks when I was 35 weeks. I couldn't look anymore. I started crying, overwhelmed with defeat. She was 11 days behind in her growth.

I drove home trying to think of something I could do to cheer myself up – but there isn't anything in the world to cheer you up when you have no control over your body failing the child growing in your belly. The next day, my doctor called and told me to be prepared to be induced at every appointment.

The following Friday, my contractions started. At first, I thought they were Braxton Hicks, but they just kept coming. By Saturday evening, I knew I was in labor and we headed to the hospital. When we arrived at the hospital, I was dilated to a three. They admitted me and hooked me up to several machines to monitor my contractions and Emersyn's heart rate. Emersyn was having late heart decels (decelerations) showing signs of stress so the doctor decided it was best if we did an emergency C-section.

I am usually a high strung nervous person – but from the moment we left the house, I was so calm. I calmed down my husband on the drive. I even asked our nurse if she was okay because she looked so flustered. I was in so much pain but just knowing Emersyn would be in my arms soon brought me so much peace.

They took me back to the operating room and gave me my spinal (epidural). My husband came in and held my hand. I was scared when they started the procedure, but soon I heard my baby girl cry!! WOW! They brought her over and showed her to me and -

♡ My heart exploded with so much love! It was like lightning struck me! ♡
♡ That moment will always be etched in my soul! Her pure perfection! ♡

Psalm 139:13-14
For you created my inmost being; you knit me together in my mother's womb. I praise you because I am fearfully and wonderfully made; your works are wonderful, I know that full well.

♡

Emersyn
and
her
amazing
Daddy

♡

My husband is the highest standard
of a dad. He expects greatness
from her, never thinking a Down
syndrome as a "can't" or "won't"
    He pushes her, and he pushes
me. When I have fears or doubts
about the future - he shoves them
all away.
    I wish the entire world could see
Down Syndrome the way he does.

Our journey to this point was long and stressful. While we were physically exhausted, Jacob and I felt confident that all the scary moments were behind us. If you are reading this, I share the challenges of my pregnancy so you can better understand my heart.

"You will face your greatest opposition when you are closest to your biggest miracle."
—Shannon L. Adler

Even though Emersyn was 5 weeks early, weighed only 4 pounds and 2 ounces, and measured 18 inches long, I had no fears. I suppose it was all the rush of endorphins – but something kept me fearless.

We tried to master the art of breastfeeding that first 24 hours with no success. She was so tired and was starting to show signs of jaundice. She went under the lights and had to stay in the NICU.

When I look back on that second day, it's like a tunnel. So strange and surreal how one minute you're just this ordinary person and then just like that, you don't even recognize yourself and how different you are than everyone else.

My mom, brother, and gramma had come to visit us and had already visited Emersyn. Jacob and I went down for her 9 am feeding. We sat there thinking how difficult this breastfeeding thing had turned out to be and that it was our greatest challenge. I so wish I could push my husband's chair closer to mine – knowing what I know now.

Our nurse came in behind our pulled curtain with the nurse practitioner. The nurse practitioner sat on the stool in front of me – and had this ominous look on her face.

It's amazing how in the most life changing moment of your life, you can't really remember all the details or spoken words. I mostly only recall all of the emotions that I was feeling when she said the words, "We *believe* Emersyn may have Down syndrome."

It's like I was on this lonely pedestal holding this perfect, tiny girl. In an instant, we were different and always will be different. My eyes stayed glued to the peaceful face – Emersyn's perfect face. Every feature they pointed out:

Palmar Crease
Almond Eyes
Small Nose
Tongue Thrust

These were all things that Jacob (husband) and I had already fallen in love with and had even credited these features to certain family members.

In a lot of ways, I decided not to believe them – and in the deepest part of my heart, I knew they were right. So many fears came flooding in –

She would never find a husband or a boyfriend.
She would never leave home.
Would she ever be able to get a job?

These fears are things I have really never chosen to talk about with anyone besides my husband, and now here I am opening my heart to anyone who wants to know – hoping it can help anyone who needs it.

I had to pull it together and hide all my emotions before we returned to my family. Somehow we convinced my brother and gramma to return home without my mom. Once we were alone, my mom looked at me expectantly. We told my mom that they think Emersyn has Down syndrome. She came rushing to me, hugging me and only saying,

"Oh Chelsey."

My mom asked Jacob to take her back one more time to see Emersyn before she went home.

I sat there, alone with my thoughts, for the first time. I heard the couple fighting in the room next to us and their baby was crying. I started sobbing uncontrollably with so many feelings of anger and jealousy. It wasn't fair! I didn't understand it. How could people like Jacob and me, who worked so hard to do everything just perfect for a healthy baby, experience this kind of challenge? And there were others who took their kids for granted and experienced no challenges. I dried up my tears before they returned, not wanting to show fear. I wanted and knew

I had to be the example for how I wanted people to feel about this diagnosis, but inside I was scared and sad.

That night, I laid in bed Googling and searching Down syndrome – trying to catch a glimpse of my future. What I found only added to my fears – health challenges, physical and mental delays, and increased chances for so many things.

Then I heard my husband snoring. He was so calm and peaceful. This diagnosis wasn't keeping him awake. And in that moment, I felt so much love come over me. God's spirit just lifted me up. I had heard people talk about feeling His power go through them, and I had always questioned it. I knew, right then, that my daughter Emersyn was going to change so many lives! She would change perspectives and hearts! For some reason, God chose Jacob and I to be the first people that she forever changed. He chose us to mold her into a person capable of so much greatness. We would get to witness every heart opening to a new world of love and would experience a new perspective of love!

I don't ever say, "God chooses special parents for special kids," because people turn down the blessing every day. But I do believe God created Emersyn specifically for me and Jacob.

Was I ready to tell everyone of her diagnosis? Absolutely not! Did I know our life would be more full than we could have ever even dreamt? YES!

The next day as we were getting ready to head down to the NICU to be with Emersyn, a nurse practitioner came into our room with the lactation consultant. It was so odd for Emersyn's doctors to come to our room. We had never even met this woman, which only made it feel more strange. Jacob and I sat on the bed while she stood over us. It felt like two children waiting for their punishment.

> "We are transferring Emersyn to OU Children's in the city. We believe she is showing signs of transient Leukemia. You should be prepared for bone marrow tests and be prepared for chemotherapy. Any questions?"'
>
> —she who must not be named

ANY QUESTIONS?????????

Yeah we had a million – no, I don't have just one!!

We thought we had experienced all the waves of trouble. But this? This was a tsunami of grief. We sat stunned and just shook our heads no.

The nurse practitioner left. The lactation consultant sat next to me and asked if there was anything she could do and if I had any questions or wanted to talk.

I exploded. I was seeing red. In these moments, your heart changes perspective forever. I told her that I knew women who had abortions because the situation was less than ideal. And here I had worked for so long to get my beautiful baby, knowing how blessed I was every single day, and I might not get to keep her???!!! Things that had nothing to do with me now seemed personal.

I called my mom and told her – they were already en route to Lawton from Ryan (70 miles) and I had to tell them to change route to OKC (130 miles). She panicked and screamed. I told her she had to calm down because I was not in a position to console her. I am an emotional person myself but somehow all I felt was rage. I suppose that was the emotion God supplied me with so I could keep it together.

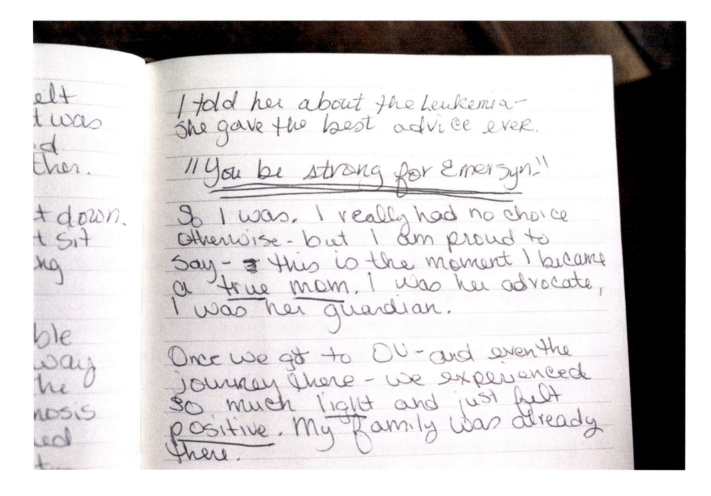

Jacob had completely shut down. All he could do was just sit in the NICU holding and loving Emersyn. Marriage is the most incredible thing. At least I feel that way about mine. The balance. The ebb and flow. During her diagnosis of Down syndrome – he soothed me and he provided the support. Now, I was picking up the slack. I called his parents so they were aware of what was happening. I called my friend Aimee. When I told her Emersyn had Down syndrome, she said, "Okay," as if I had told her that the sky is blue. She didn't flinch. You can imagine my relief at not hearing the big disappointment in "I'm sorry."

I told her about the Leukemia and she gave the best advice ever – "You be strong for Emersyn." So I was. I really had no choice otherwise. But I am proud to say – this is the moment I became a true mom. I was Emersyn's advocate. I was her guardian.

Once we got to OU, and even during the journey there, we experienced so much light and felt so positive. My family was already there. My mom had waited by the elevator. When the team came out to take Emersyn to the NICU, my mom said, "Is that Emersyn? I am her Grammy!" It was as if she were saying, "We expect y'all to take the best care of her because she is so loved!" My Mom provided us with so much love and support during this time.

Emersyn wasn't eating much so they put in a feeding tube. We met the doctor and instantly felt trust and relief. Within a matter of 3 days, we had been told there was no longer a concern for Leukemia. Emersyn had a few mild heart defects that would most likely resolve and one heart defect, a bicuspid aortic valve, that we would need to watch but it wasn't a huge concern at this point in her life.

It was an absolute miracle for us. We had so many people praying for Emersyn. It can seem lonely in the hospital at times, but I know now that we were never alone. Our entire church came together to pray over Emersyn. Our tiny 4 pound girl already changed an entire community.

We stayed in the NICU at OU for 9 days. The doctors thought we would be there an additional 2 weeks – but Jacob, Emersyn, and I worked hard and were able to go home (with 25 cups of breastmilk, might I add).

We decided Emersyn's theme from Day 1 was – Expect the Unexpected.

My quad screen was negative. Gestational diabetes gives big babies, but Emersyn was tiny. She surprised doctors – already in her small time of 2 weeks. She liked kangaroo care on her back.

Oklahoma Down Syndrome Festival 2015

For one so small
You seem so strong
My arms will hold you
Keep you safe and warm
This bond between us
Can't be broken
I will be here
Don't you cry
'Cause you'll be in my heart

—From Tarzan

Emersyn is now 2 years old. From a medical standpoint, she has hypothyroidism, she wears glasses (sometimes), and she will always have a bicuspid aortic valve.

We have 5 therapists, all of whom I consider to be friends. We are so lucky to have such incredible people in our life. In the beginning, I hated that she needed therapy and it made me sad that Jacob and I weren't enough for her. Now, I know that it is a blessing to have more people love and influence your child's growth – physically AND socially.

She is rowdy and sassy, and just like any 2 year old, she can throw a huge tantrum.

We went through so many scares and trials in the beginning of her life. We now know Down syndrome isn't scary. What is terrifying, is not having her here with us.

The truth is there are hard times, yes. There are times you see other children and will realize how far behind your child is and it just plain sucks!

But then you look over and see that smile – SO BRIGHT!

Times that she learns something new, showing us the payoff of our hard work.

The hate you have for low-tone, until she gives that hug that just melts into you.

The trusting look she gives us through blood work or a doctor's visit.

How only people she loves are lucky enough to receive those amazing gifts.

The way SO many people want to be a part of her world.

You know that YOU are the lucky one.

She has taught us it's okay to have faith and to believe in miracles BIG and SMALL!

My husband is the highest standard of a dad. He expects greatness from her, never thinking of Down syndrome as a "can't" or "won't." He pushes her and he pushes me. When I have fears or doubts about the future, he shoves them all away.

I wish the entire world could see Down syndrome the way he sees Down syndrome.

She is my reason for everything in this world.

I could never thank God enough for giving her to me.

Psalm 59:16
But I will sing of your strength, in the morning. I will sing of your love; for you are my fortress, my refuge in times of trouble.

The Elder Family
Everything is better in Emersyn's World!

In closing, I know these things to be true:

Nobody knows my child the way that I know my child.

All of my initial fears are completely gone. I have seen and heard too many accounts of individuals with Down syndrome to believe otherwise. And even if I hadn't — why can't my daughter be the one to pave the way for others?

People are ignorant at times and it will hurt. All you need to do to wash away all of that pain is simple — look at that precious child who loves and adores you.

Love is a many-splendored thing. It lifts us up where we belong. All you need is LOVE.

2021 update: Emersyn is now 7 and is a big sister! She has a very energetic little brother named Luca, who is 4 years old. He has added so much flavor and made our family even more unique in ways we didn't even think possible! They have a very sweet relationship that needs no words at all. Emersyn thinks she is his boss and a lot of the time she is actually being very helpful. She also makes sure everyone acknowledges Luca if they've spoken to her as she wants everyone to know he is her brother.

Emersyn has also since been diagnosed with Type 1 diabetes, which has been a very big challenge for our family. It is such a complicated and scary disease, causing so much fear for the future. But we have been so lucky that Emersyn is so brave, adaptable, and she just keeps shining so bright.

If I'm writing this to myself in 2013, holding precious baby Emersyn, I would tell myself that she is an old soul. At the age of 7, she will have so much empathy. Without a word, she will know when you're upset and ask if you're okay. She will be so caring and you will be so proud of her. She will love playing video games and acting out song and dance theatrics from all of her favorite movies. She will teach you so much more about compassion, empathy and joy than you ever knew possible.

She flipped every perspective on life. The world is new and beautiful with her in it.
It's Emersyn's World.

Chelsey Elder

Instagram: chelsey.elder
Emersynsworld.blogspot.com

The Elder Family

Everything's better in
Emersyn's World!

Christine & Emma

"In those first two months I changed. Emma had already brought
out a person I never knew existed until I became her mom."

—Christine DeFroy

Emma Grace Hemrick

"Though she be but little, she is fierce!" – William Shakespeare

October 19, 2013
1:03am
6lbs, 3oz – 19 inches
Greensboro, NC

Journal Entry by mom, Christine.
Written March 7, 2016

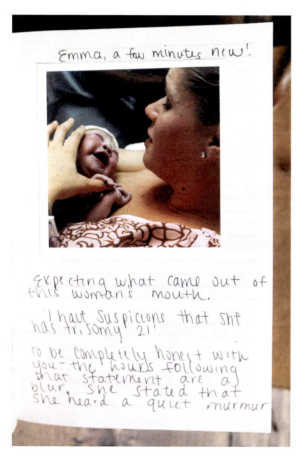

Emma, a few minutes new!

On a warm October day in 2013, my life was forever changed – I became a mother!

With that comes a whole new lifestyle and a whole lot of unknowns. Unbeknownst to me at the time of Emma's arrival was just how much unknown this new bundle of joy held.

The morning after she was born, the on-call pediatrician looked at us over the top of Emma's plastic hospital bassinet. She had been to the hospital the night Emma was born and had already checked her out so I wasn't really expecting what came out of her mouth next.

"I have suspicions that she has Trisomy 21."

To be completely honest with you, the hours following that statement are a blur. She stated that she heard a quiet murmur in her heart and a cardiologist would be in to examine her. She left Emma's dad and I alone in the room with our beautiful new baby and a whole lot of doubt, suspicions, and fear. We actually didn't believe her. She didn't spend much time trying to explain her suspicions and we were very confused and felt very alone.

The series of events that followed are a bit scrambled in my memory. Family came. Gifts were opened and tears were shed. Emma was snuggled constantly. I didn't want to put her down. Finally, a cardiologist came and took her for an EKG and an ECHO – an ultrasound of her heart. When he returned he didn't have good news – Emma had a very large VSD (Ventricular Septal Defect) and two small ASDs, holes in her heart. We were told that she'd probably need open heart surgery. I begged him to tell me his opinion of her having Down syndrome since we still were not convinced. He told us that based on her physical characteristics and her heart defects, he was 90% certain that she had Down syndrome.

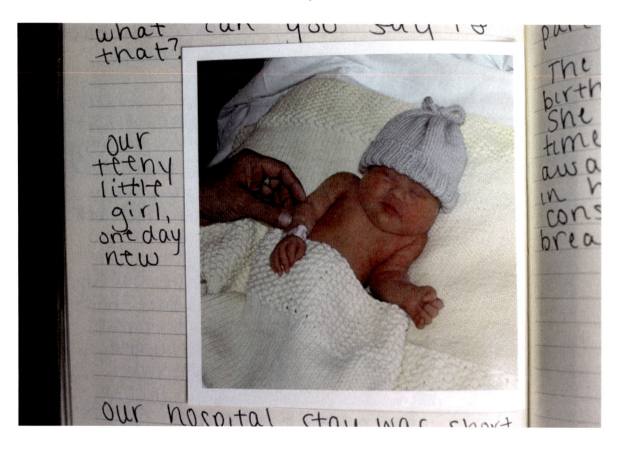

It seemed like before I could process that, someone else was in our room explaining that Emma was jaundice and needed light therapy. She had arrived unexpectedly almost four weeks before her due date and jaundice is common with earlier births. They brought in a breast pump to start trying to get her to eat, breastfeeding was something I really wanted to do but she was having so much trouble latching. At that point, I do remember telling everyone that no one else was allowed to come or go because every time our door opened more bad news came. I needed time. I wanted time alone with my little girl. To hold her and to bond with her. At that point, that's all that mattered to me. Of course I didn't get my wish, there were so many blood draws, temperature checks, constant in and out, and Emma being taken from me for various reasons. One nurse kept asking me if I was ok and if I needed anything – what can you say to that??

Our hospital stay was luckily short. We left three days after I had Emma. All the things I was prepared to feel or experience with my new baby were totally different than the reality. We left the hospital with not only Emma but so much medical equipment! A light therapy blanket, a rented breast pump, different medications to help with her heart defects, appointments scheduled with specialists, and two totally unprepared parents. To say we were overwhelmed was an understatement!

The month following Emma's arrival was a terrifying learning curve. She had such a difficult time feeding and staying awake due to her holes in her heart. I was constantly watching her breathing and documenting every ounce of milk she drank, sometimes only a milliliter at a time. Open heart surgery was on the horizon, but she ideally needed to gain some weight. I spent so much time and effort keeping her alive that I don't really remember much else about that time but being constantly worried.

While I struggled with finally receiving the bloodwork confirmation of her extra chromosome and the diagnosis of Down syndrome, what was mostly at the forefront of my mind was keeping her healthy, comfortable, and basically alive until her cardiologist was ready to move forward with surgery.

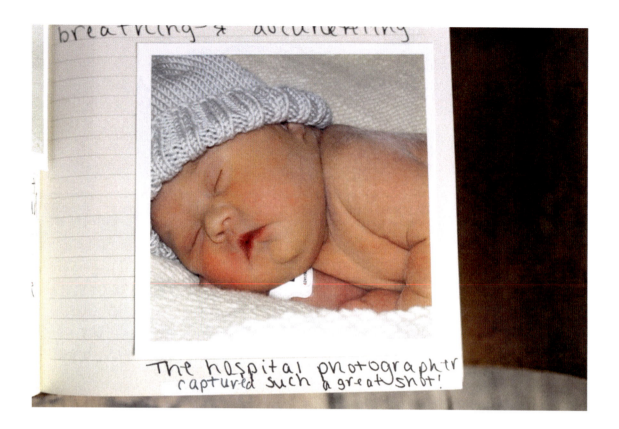

The hospital photographer captured such a great shot!

During her first two months of life, I did a lot of thinking – about what our lives would hold, how my thoughts and dreams for my daughter's life had changed so drastically and so quickly. There were good times and there were hard times. I was thankful for a healthy pregnancy and a safe and uneventful delivery. We had chosen not to do any prenatal testing during the pregnancy, and for me I was happy to have had a stress-free and very easy nine months carrying her. Honestly, I was so focused on keeping Emma alive those first two months that I didn't have a lot of extra worry about other challenges that still would lie ahead.

In those first two months I changed. Emma had already brought out a person I never knew existed until I became her mom. Some refer to this as "momma bear." Once a meek, quiet person who quickly agreed to appease everyone, I became a loud, speak up for your child advocate for this tiny little girl who couldn't yet advocate for herself. Will, Emma's dad, was always calm, always asking the questions I never thought to ask. It was hard for me to argue with doctors, but we always knew our daughter best. I struggled with her cardiologist. He didn't listen to me. I expressed concerns every week in his office about her sleeping seventeen to twenty hours a day (his response – babies sleep). I expressed concerns about her drinking a half an ounce at a feeding (his response – kids with Down syndrome don't drink well). He kept dragging his feet and postponing surgery and using her extra chromosome as an excuse rather than listening to me. Eventually a formula to supplement my pumped breast milk was introduced by the same cardiologist even though she was hardly drinking an ounce at a time. He was more focused on weight gain than anything else. The formulas (we tried a couple) caused Emma to projectile vomit. I will never forget Emma's dad looking at the cardiologist and saying, "She's not going to gain weight if she's vomiting so please let's drop the formula." (Why did we even have to point that out to him?!) Her pediatrician had even suggested starting her on a reflux medicine to counteract the issues with the formula. I was so upset, thinking of another medication to add to this tiny little 6 pound baby, when she was actually doing really well just drinking the breast milk I so lovingly pumped every 3-4 hours, round the clock. I felt so out of control and helpless with everything else with Emma, so pumping that milk for her felt like the only thing I could practically do to help her.

Emma's first moments home - meeting her 'big brother' Jack :)

We had so many doctor appointments and so many differing opinions. I was so weary with the entire medical community. I was exhausted and felt as if I was single-handedly keeping my daughter alive hour by hour at this point. Emma had her two month check up the day before her first Christmas Eve. We had just been to the cardiologist three days prior for her weekly check. Her early interventionist had been to the house that week as well and had commented on her color being pale. It was not just me who was noticing that she was not feeling well. Alas, again, despite my concerns of just how much she was sleeping, he didn't think it necessary for us to do an EKG. That day of her check up, her pediatrician noticed Emma's respiratory rate was high and she was breathing very laboriously. She sent us directly home with instructions to pack our bags and prepare for a hospital stay. Before we had made it home she called to say we needed to take her directly to Duke University Hospital. We were scared, worried, and just wanted to get Emma healthy.

We were very fortunate for a lot – her pediatrician's thorough examination that day, my parents being in town for Christmas, a highly regarded surgeon who just happened to be on rotations that holiday week, and an incredible staff of nurses who came up with nicknames and loved our daughter as much as we did. We were fortunate for a stronger, healthier, and definitely hungrier little girl post surgery! We also have since changed cardiologists. The one Emma had been followed by since her birth never even checked up on her while she was in the hospital for surgery or recovering.

Emma hasn't had many other big issues health wise outside of her surgery. She just got tubes put in her ears and her adenoids removed, which paled in comparison to the heart surgery. The adenoid removal was a game changer – we learned post-op that they were blocking 90% of her breathing!

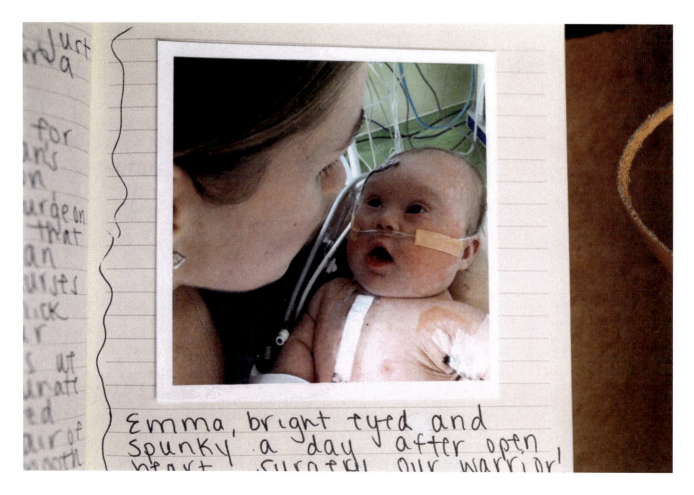

Emma, bright eyed and spunky a day after open heart surgery. Our warrior!

Trying to put Emma and her incredible personality into words is next to impossible. She is our bright star, our sunshine. She brings such light to everyone she meets.

Looking back almost two and a half years later now, it's sad to remember how upset and scared we were. The unknown is always scary but when you're also new parents, everything is heightened. But you know what? No one has all the answers. No one can predict the future. And trying to do that gets you nowhere fast.

We had denied any prenatal testing because again, you cannot predict the future. No test offered to us would definitively tell us who our baby would be. It seemed like an added stress. Looking back, I am so happy with that decision. Having Emma to hold and love on and smell her sweet baby smell was all the reassurance I needed during that scary time.

To all of the new parents, either prenatally diagnosed or directly following birth, know how OK this is. How amazingly OK this is. How your child will flourish with your love, grow and learn, and be your biggest proudest accomplishment. How they will make you laugh, cry, and drive you crazy, like any other child does. One of the best pieces of advice I got was from Emma's amazing early interventionist, the week after Emma was born. I had looked at her through tear-stained eyes and said, "How do I do this?" Her response? She said, "Christine, you just had a baby. Love her, hold her, and treat her like a newborn baby." So simple yet so important. Sweet momma, if you're reading this, you just gave birth or you just got a prenatal diagnosis. Celebrate that, enjoy that, and love that baby! You've been given an incredible gift. Do not let anyone, no doctor, no nurse, tell you to do otherwise. I now grieve for all of the time I spent grieving. So silly and naive of me to think I somehow lost out on something when I learned about her diagnosis. We are the lucky ones to have this beautiful perfect angel who has taught us more in her two and a half years than I feel like I will ever teach her. She is sassy, determined, smart, funny… I could go on and on…you see where I'm going with this.

For Emma's second christmas,
she got a baby brother :)

the very large and very
awesome local Down
syndrome group here in
town. We've made many
friends and have learned
so much.

Like any families, we have
ups and hard times and
yes times get difficult.
But having so much

I am so proud of the toddler she has become. We do speech therapy, physical therapy, and occupational therapy. We are involved with the very large and very awesome local Down syndrome group here in town. We've made many friends and have learned so much!

Like any family, we have ups and hard times and yes times get difficult. But having so much support from the local network, her therapists, and family, it's easy to see how bright Emma's future truly is.

The advice I leave you with is always advocate, advocate, advocate. Listen to your heart and never take no for an answer. You have just been given an incredible and priceless gift. Congratulations.

Love,

Emma, Greyson, and Christine

IG: cmarie1008

03/13/2021 Update

Emma is an independent, opinionated, and hilarious 7 year old. She loves to dance, listen to music, and make people laugh. Her smile is infectious and she is an amazing big sister to Greyson; her very supportive, caring, and loving little brother. They are only 14 months apart and are truly the best of friends. Watching their relationship grow over the years and seeing the things they both learn from one another are truly my greatest gifts as their mother. When I was not yet a mother, a teacher by trade and at heart, I was so excited about teaching my children everything. I had no idea at the time just how naive that thought was. The life lessons and viewpoint on life that I have after having children and experiencing life through Emma's eyes are things that can never be learned from a textbook or in an 'ordinary' life. This extraordinary journey was something that I was once terrified of embarking on. There have been hard times, and I'm sure more to come, but the hills are so much greater than those valleys. The hills are where the sun shines the brightest, the flowers smell the sweetest, and the grass is actually greener. Families like ours, we truly get to see the sharpest colors and the biggest celebrations. Things are appreciated more and your entire perspective of life gets shifted. Most importantly, you're never alone in your journey. The families that walked before us, the families that will walk after us. We're all part of a bigger family. Welcome to the family.

support from the local network, her therapists and family, its easy to see how bright Emma's future truly is.

The advice I leave you with is always advocate, advcate, advocate. Listen to your heart

and never take no for an answer. Love, Emma, Greyson, Will & Christine
IG: cmarie1008

Abigail & David

Abigail Sacran mom to David
New Albany, MS
June 30, 2016

David Ewing Sacran

For this child we have PRAYED

"I felt an overwhelming sense of guilt – I loved David. He was
my child, but the reality of my new life was difficult. Then slowly...
day by day, the clouds gave way to SUNSHINE."

—Abigail Sacran

Abigail Sacran – mom to David
New ALbany, MS
June 30, 2016

I am the 19th person to write in this diary. It's surreal, overwhelming to think that this diary has through 18 homes, lives, hands. We all are walking an unexpected journey, but our experiences are the same – this detour of our life has become one of our greatest blessings. If you are reading the pages of this diary the chances are that your life is beginning a journey you never expected. I hope our story, our family, our sunshine will bring you hope, happiness, and encouragement.

My husband, Louis, and I prayed for a child for a year and a half before we found out we were expecting our second child. We were thrilled, excited, and thankful. Our three year old, Lily, was happy she would be a big sister and soon began calling the baby "sunshine." For 9 months we called the baby Sunshine. After a normal, healthy pregnancy I gave birth to David Ewing Sacran. A 7lb, 7oz baby boy. Shortly after birth the baby was taken to the NICU because his oxygen was too low and a few hours later David began turning blue around his mouth when he cried. The next few days proved to be the longest, darkest days that I had ever experienced. The morning after David was born, a pediatrician sat down on my hospital bed, took my hand and said, "We suspect your baby has a congenital heart disease (CHD)." I held her hand and wept – as a mother my biggest fear was coming to pass. They performed an echocardiogram on David's heart and a cardiologist from LeBonheur Children's Hospital came to give us a CHD diagnosis of Complete AV Canal. My baby would need open heart surgery. My world was slowly caving in. I was trying to hold it together and be strong as Lily arrived to see her "SUNSHINE."

arrived to see her "SUNSHINE."

It was determined that David would need a level 4 NICU, so he was transferred to LeBonheur's Children's Hospital in Memphis, Tennessee. A few hours later I was able to join David and Louis. I cried as my husband wheeled me into David's NICU room. There he was, my new baby, not even a day old with wires, needles, and medicine. My heart broke. Our admitting nurse was an angel, and I often thank God that He gave her to us. Part of the hospital admission process is to receive informative paperwork on your child's medical condition. The nurse handed me the info on David's heart defect – there on the front page: "50% of children born with this defect have Down syndrome." I walked over to David's bed and tears began to fall. I could see it in his almond eyes. I didn't ask about Down syndrome because I didn't want to know. Instead, I kicked back in the green hospital recliner, ate steak, and held my sweet sunshine skin to skin. He was mine, and he was perfect.

The next morning, I was sitting in that same green recliner holding David when a geneticist came into our NICU room. I will never forget her words or that moment. "Let me eyeball this baby," she says. "Yes, I agree with the doctors this baby has Down syndrome." The tears immediately began to fall as I looked up at my husband and took his hand. Our first born son, the one to carry on the family name had an extra chromosome. Louis looked at me, wiped a few tears from his face, and said, "I'm not upset about this." My husband, Lily and David's father, has still never said a word or shown an emotion to contradict that statement.

I felt different. I was upset. I was angry. How could this happen? I was 32, healthy – my baby had no markers in the womb. The nurse who we had for the day was thrilled for us. She beamed with excitement as she told us how she and her husband had prayed that their last baby would have Down syndrome, and when the baby was born typical they wanted to adopt a child with Down syndrome. I sat in my green chair and thought she was crazy, but as time passed I began to hear more and more stories like this one...individuals whose lives had been so affected by those with DS that they wanted to adopt someone with Down syndrome in their family. I would learn, slowly learn, that David's nurse and so many others weren't crazy after all and that the little boy I cuddled would become my greatest joy and blessing.

The fact that David had DS began to fade into the background as we began to face additional health problems. David had not had a dirty

diaper and by the end of the day 2 of the doctors became concerned that he had a medical condition preventing him from having a bowel movement. We had to discontinue his feeds, begin him on TPN (total parenteral nutrition which involves nutrients given by IV), and insert a tube down his throat and into his stomach to continuously suction bile that he couldn't digest. We hoped and prayed for a simple solution, but a biopsy of his lower intestines proved that our sunshine, only 4 days old, had Hirschsprung's Disease. This disease disables the ability to stool because part of the colon is dead. When David was 9 days old he had a successful pull-through surgery that allowed him to poo. I have never been <u>so</u> happy to see poo! Our NICU stay continued for 5 more weeks as we waited for David to learn to eat. Baby Boy could not go home until he could eat enough calories without working his heart too much. When Sunshine was 6 weeks old we left the hospital to take him home and join Lily.

I was happy to be home, to be reunited with Lily, but the reality of my life was staring me in the face. I was home with a child who had Down syndrome. He was not the boy I had imagined for 9 months. I spent my days and nights caring for a child with a serious heart condition and praying to God that he didn't develop congestive heart failure before he needed open heart surgery. I cried often and battled guilt over the thoughts and feelings I had.

David had open heart surgery when he was 3 months old. He did amazing, and we were home within 5 days. HOME, my life was settling down. My baby's heart was fixed. Now what? I wish I could tell you how easily I accepted this new life – a life of doctor's appointments and therapy and the many extra things that go along with having a baby with Down syndrome. This new life was one I never expected, never wanted. Some days my grief and sadness consumed me. I felt an overwhelming sense of guilt – I loved David. He was my child, but the reality of my new life was difficult. Then slowly...day by day, the clouds gave way to SUNSHINE.

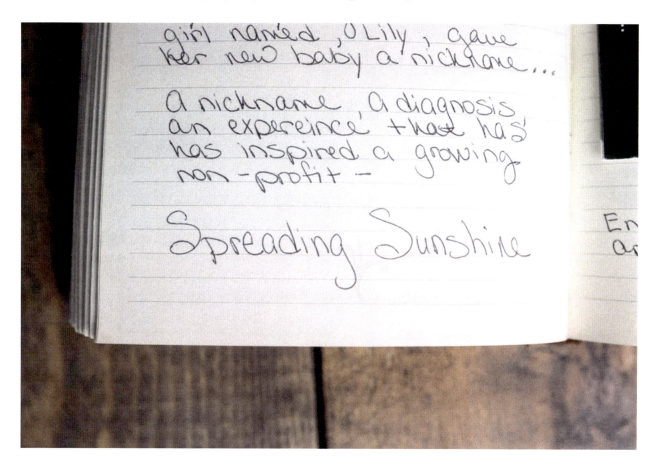

Beautiful, beautiful sunshine. The fears of the unknown and the future, the sadness that I felt, the worry over what others thought began to disappear. David was mine. He belonged to me, and he was fearfully and wonderfully made. This little boy began to teach me so many lessons – lessons about myself, others, life. I began to see the world with a new perspective. My fear (yes, I'm embarrassed to say it) of others with disabilities no longer existed, because I began to see and understand that these individuals are no different than me. I wish I could go back to those first days and tell myself not to be sad, to not cry and worry. The months that were wasted in sadness were difficult but unnecessary. I wish I could have known what a truly beautiful gift I had been given. A gift I would have never asked for, but a gift that has changed my life forever. David's life is one of my greatest blessings.

One little boy sparked a movement…

Enjoy your new beautiful, amazing life. ♡ Abigail

Here I am (not in my green chair:-)) 3 years later, and Sunshine continues to bring us unimaginable joy and happiness. We just celebrated his 3rd birthday, cheered as he has mastered walking, and are overjoyed that he will be a big brother this Fall.

My story ends with how my story began. A little girl named Lily, gave her new baby a nickname…

A nickname, a diagnosis, an experience that has inspired a growing non-profit –

Spreading Sunshine

Enjoy your new, beautiful, amazing life.

Love Abigail

A movement of light and joy for families facing childhood illnesses and disabilities. A movement called **Spreading Sunshine**.

Before David was born, his big sister Lily nicknamed him Sunshine. As it turned out, when he was diagnosed with Down syndrome and a heart defect his nickname proved to be perfect. David is truly Sunshine to all who meet him, but especially to his parents, Abigail and Louis. Abigail says, "David's life has taught us to see with new eyes and new perspective. There are so many families and children who need support, love, encouragement, and sunshine."

In July 2014 David's family heard of a little girl in Pennsylvania who was having open heart surgery, so they sent her a *Sunshine Box* filled with items to brighten her day. Other people read what they had done on David's Facebook page and wanted to join and help.

Since that time volunteers have sent over fifteen-hundred sunshine boxes to families in all fifty states and fifteen countries. Each *Sunshine Box* is uniquely put together and shipped by the volunteer. Boxes have been sent to children who were surgery patients, or who had heart disease, cerebral palsy, kidney disease, mitochondrial disease, seizures, and neurological disorders.

Spreading Sunshine is a nonprofit organization mobilizing volunteers to encourage and support families facing childhood illnesses or disabilities.

Care is shown care by meeting practical and emotional needs of families through sunshine boxes, gift cards for meals, lockets for grieving mothers, and hospital care packages.

Compassion flows from our own experiences and from hearts filled with love for the families we serve.

Community is built through one-on-one relationships and through a private online community of support for our volunteers and families.

Join the Movement
Visit **spreading-sunshine.com** to learn how your child can become a sunshine buddy or how you can help us scatter sunshine.

Michelle & Mara

"From the moment we knew Mara had Down syndrome, my only fear has been how society will affect the way she feels about herself."

—Michelle Clark

Michelle Clark
Wilburton, Cambridge, United Kingdom
October, 2016

Caption: Mara Jaye Clark
Born June 2012

I began scrawling some notes in preparation for our contribution over a year ago, there are just two I want to include now I finally have ink flowing …

It's Friday. On Wednesday, Ben said to me:
"Tonight as I watched Mara engrossed in a movie, all I saw was my beautiful daughter. That's the first time I've done that."
Mara was 3 years and two months old.

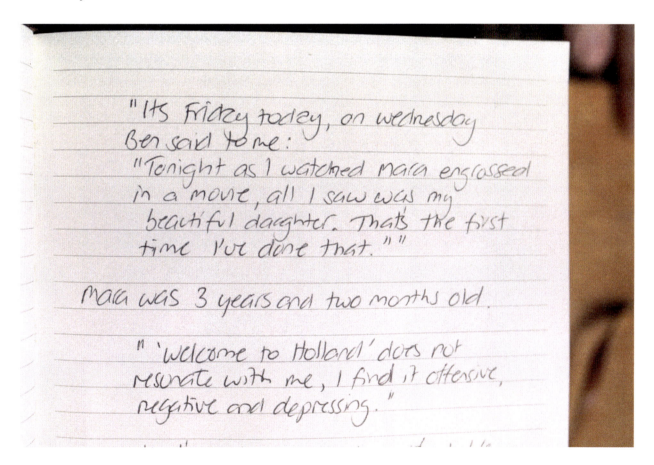

"'Welcome to Holland' does not resonate with me, I find it offensive, negative, and depressing."

Well that's putting my cards on the table. Gulp.

I remember being ever so happy that Ben finally saw Mara, and also so sad that he had not seen what I had for the first 3 years of her life. I wondered if Mara had missed out on something, and indeed Ben, because he was unable for that time to see her as a whole. It's obvious that he's loved her since we knew we were pregnant, this did not change when we received her diagnosis, his view of her has always been honest and reflected his own life's conditionings, thoughts, and feelings.

It didn't mean he loved her less, or more, his perspective was just different. And it's ok to be different.

Ben & Mara's relationship, the bond they share, it's so incredibly beautiful and impossible to put into words. I feel unbelievably fortunate to witness this develop and feel an enormous sense of pride for both Ben and Mara.

When Jamie asked if I'd contribute to this diary we were just two years into our journey. I learnt much in those first two years, much more since and undoubtedly will continue to do so as I grow with Mara.

What I know is simply this – our experience is our own. There may be similarities, occasional instances where our experiences cross, and times where they seem to run in parallel, but our journeys will not be the same. Our Mara is our Mara. Your child will be your child. A diagnosis does not define my child, or our family, nor will it yours.

At what point we received Mara's diagnosis, what decisions we made along the way or how she arrived in this world is all very interesting, but all that actually matters is that she's here, and she is loved, immeasurably.

7 weeks early and tiny, but breathing on her own. Both holes in her heart closed naturally within 18 months and she continues to have sleep apnea, constipation, and bouts of croup.

Her tonsils and adenoids were removed six months ago and this has helped enormously with her sleep apnea and congestion. In fact, it's changed her life. Her constipation is managed with medication and a high intake of fluids.

Mara is sensitive to some noise situations; an espresso machine in a cafe, music in the arcades at the seaside, the bustle at a train station, and we've found ear defenders make anywhere and everything accessible.

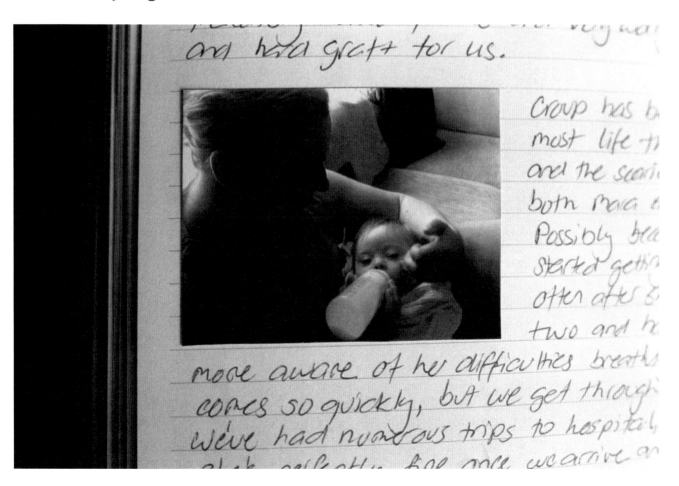

Mara's ankles both turn in and she has a very high instep. For this she wears orthotics and requires ankle support from her shoes so it limits her style options. I had a similar issue when I was young.

For Mara, it's the congestion and constipation that's specifically related to her Down syndrome and I won't sugar coat it, at times the effects of these conditions have been incredibly horrid for her and very worrying and challenging for us.

Croup has been the most life threatening and the scariest for both Mara and I. Possibly because she started getting it more often after she was two and has been more aware of her difficulties breathing. It comes so quickly, but we get through it. We've had numerous trips to hospital, some she's perfectly fine once we arrive and we appear overly anxious parents, and others where she wouldn't have survived had we not made that call. It's a bizarre realization when you're holding your child in an ambulance struggling to take a breath and all the time you're hoping desperately for disapproving tutts from medical staff upon arrival because it appears you've wasted their time.

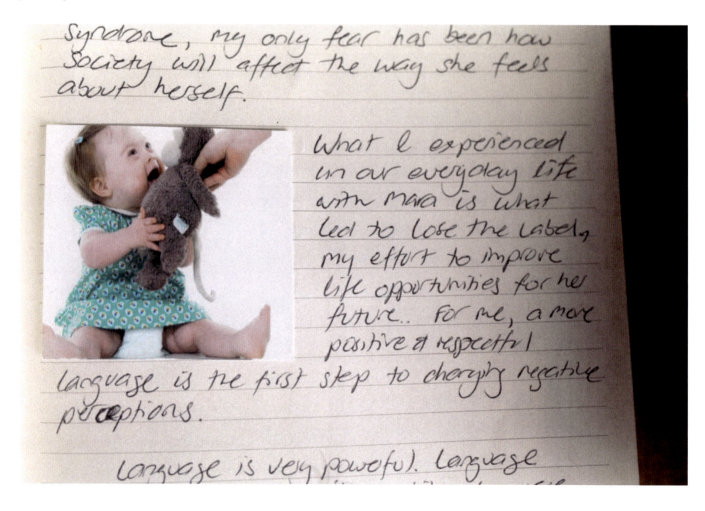

Syndrome, my only fear has been how society will affect the way she feels about herself.

What I experienced in our everyday life with Mara is what led to Lose the Label, my effort to improve life opportunities for her future. For me, a more positive & respectful language is the first step to changing negative perceptions.

Language is very powerful. Language

What I've found most difficult is society's perceptions and the negative and defining language it uses that fuels them. From the moment we knew Mara has Down syndrome, my only fear has been how society will affect the way she feels about herself.

What I experienced in our everyday life with Mara is what led me to Lose the Label, my effort to improve life opportunities for the Down syndrome community. For me, language aligned with the fact that we are all of equal value is crucial in changing perceptions.

> "Language is very powerful. Language does not just describe reality. Language creates the reality it describes."
>
> —Desmond Tutu

All I can contribute to this diary, to your journey, is to share a little of my life with Mara and my continued work for all. The best advocate for Mara, is Mara, but she's as yet unskilled in the art of communication.

Everything is relative. Our life is everything we make it, my relationship with Ben, with Mara, with our family and friends. Life did not stop because my child has Down syndrome, it took a new path because I became Mara's mother and what I've learned along the way is down to that. I became a mother, to my child.

We celebrated Mara's 4th birthday in June with a beach party. Yellow spades, beach balls and blankets, and a sandcastle for a birthday cake (we didn't eat it!). Mara was beaming. And so was I. This was the first time she had been able to communicate her choice of birthday activity to us and I can't explain how wonderful the day was because of it.

I'm not sure if it's because milestones are harder won, or achieved outside the typical time-lines that helps us appreciate them more, or because of her diagnosis we make it a priority to learn the skills to help her achieve each step and possibly, just possibly, it's an individual and personal win for us too, for putting in what's considered that "extra effort." It may be because the majority of what we hear from the point of diagnosis is so negative, so life lim-iting, and we're standing there witnessing the opposite unfold everyday in our own child. I don't know, just thoughts…the excitement with each milestone achieved is so real and intense.

Mara is an incredibly determined character, it is her making and her danger. She's highly mo-tivated, can be hilariously funny and has acquired many of my personal traits – and not just the good ones!

Mara, is Mara, but shes as yet unskilled in the art of writing.

Everything is relative. Our life is everything we make it, my relationship with Ben, with Mara, with our family et friends. Life did not stop because my child has Downs

She can be as chilled as her Dad and tune me out when focused on the TV or her iPad. She loves days out most but is happy at home hanging out with "the olds".

Mara can be very animated and her focus on the relationships between characters in movies is amazingly beautiful to watch. She delights in scooping water out of her bath with an incredibly accurate aim – and with such speed it's a constant reminder that we really need a wet room!

This month's music selection is the Hokey Cokey and Shawn Mendez's "Stitches." It's easy to assume she knows all the moves to Hokey Cokey, and for "Stitches" Mara throws herself on the floor and lies herself across the bonnet of her pedal car mimicking the music video clip with impeccable timing.

Mara started in reception year at school in September and she absolutely loves it. She's thriving. She's learning at an incredible pace, her speech leaves us gasping, she's participating, building relationships with her teachers and friendships with her peers. We have a daily communication book that tells us what she's enjoyed that day and also what she's found challenging. So far, nothing more than tidying up or coming inside from outdoor play. There will be challenges that come, but for now she's doing just great.

Mara is a little girl, one with her own character, her own strengths, joys, and frustrations. Her diagnosis, the fact that she has Down syndrome does not define any of this. It plays a part, but by no means is it, or will it ever become who she is.

She's in my heart, and she engulfs it.

Enjoy your journey, I hope it's as beautiful as mine.

2021 Update:

Mara reminds us daily that she'll soon be 9 and in amongst the joys of life with this phenomenally expressive, theatrical, audience demanding performer and comedian, the years have brought a generous share of anxieties and challenging behaviours which retrospectively, have been due to inadequacies of provision at school. Sometimes it's been me, too tired to have the patience needed in that moment, or focusing on other essential priorities, hey, I'm human, and the constant fight for her human rights, her education, and services can be exhausting.

We've had Mara at home like many in England since March 2020 (Covid-19), just gone a year now, for which I'm incredibly grateful. This unexpected time together has afforded the opportunity to see very clearly, the environment Mara needs for optimised learning, so we've been making changes to ensure she gets just that and its success is already evident. I'm so incredibly proud of her, you know that overwhelming pride, the one that's hard to say without welling up? Yeah, that pride.

Wendy, Mike & Oliver

"I wanted to tell you these stories because no one was able to tell me anything positive when Oliver was born and diagnosed. I simply sat weeping on my own in that little hospital room holding my baby."

—Wendy O'Carroll

Wendy, Mike, Oliver, and Anna
Somerset, England UK
December 2016/January 2017

Life is a Journey.

Hello you, I'm Wendy. As I put these words together, I find myself wondering who you are and why you are reading my story. I imagine that you are a new parent seeking comfort, reassurance and information. Or maybe you are further along in your parenting journey and are in need of a little inspiration. Perhaps you are a professional looking to gather more knowledge to better support the parents you work with. Or perhaps you are a friend or an extended family member who wants to better inform themselves and their loved ones. Whoever you are, I wish I could be with you now, enjoying a cup of tea (and perhaps a Coke) and sharing everything that I have learned.

I'm aware that I can't magically transport you to my home, where I could slowly open up this amazing world for you. As I find my words and put my thoughts together, I feel like the best audience for my story is the "new parent." I wish I could give you the comfort you need right now. I know it can be scary but I want to reassure you that it is honestly going to be ok. I know your journey will be different than you planned and there will be some challenging times, but you are going to love this child more than you could ever imagine. The connection I have with my son Oliver runs from the deepest part of my soul to the deepest part of his. Our connection is so strong, incredible and utterly glorious. I can assure you that the reality is that having a child with or without Down syndrome can be a challenge. My amazing daughter Anna, who was eight years old when Oliver was born, is the first to admit that she can be more difficult than her brother.

neices too. I love my Dad, and my sister - me and my sister like to go out - we have 'brother sister' days. I like those. Oh and my mother - well - she's awesome - well - most of the time ....."

Oliver winning the 'National Diversity Award' for 'UK Positive Role Model for Disability' in 2015.

Oliver with his beloved 'neices'♥

They adore him ♥♥

(Mike's grand-daughters)

In the beginning, much of what you may feel is sadness, unhappiness and dissatisfaction. You may believe that the hopes and dreams you had for your child have vanished or are shattered. The process is similar to looking at a beautiful stained glass window – all the thoughts and visions you've had for your child about who he or she would become creates the stained glass pattern. Then, someone comes along with a huge placard that reads "DOWN SYNDROME" and suddenly, your window shatters. Now all you see are the broken remains of your beautiful and unique window on the floor, along with a large, ugly sign that so blatantly spells out something you don't want to see. How could "something like this" happen to you?

The reality is that nothing has shattered, the pattern has simply changed. Your fear and worries are based on not knowing about the journey that lies ahead of you. Perhaps you have snippets of information about Down syndrome, or maybe you once read an article that caught your eye. Fear of the unknown can be difficult but EVERYONE experiences it. You are not alone in your fear.

I have read all the entries in this diary so far, and I'm aware that the vast majority of the stories are written by parents of younger children with Down syndrome. I think as a new parent, that is probably what you need most. I'm also aware that we as parents tend to start looking and worrying about what lies ahead for our children when they become young adults. We can let our minds become overrun with fears that our children will be unable to function, achieve or enjoy life as we do. Well, just so you know THAT SIMPLY ISN'T TRUE!!

I don't need to describe the heartbreak and despair of the diagnosis and those early days because other lovely and amazing parents in this diary have already bared their souls so eloquently. YES, THERE WERE CHALLENGES AND STRUGGLES. Oliver underwent open heart surgery at three and a half months old and he was diagnosed with severe hypotonia (very poor muscle tone) which led his physiotherapist to predict that he would be unable to do sports. His speech pathologist diagnosed him with verbal dyspraxia and said it was likely his speech would never be clear enough to be understood by an unfamiliar listener.

I happen to be a very awkward yet determined woman, so when someone tells me something can't be done, I just have to SHOW them that it can be!! So I came up with different types of activities, strategies, etc., to help Oliver be the best he could be — and he is indeed amazing!! He was skateboarding at eight years old, and he has been interviewed on both radio and television regarding his photography. He has a great vocabulary and is more than capable of making himself understood.

For instance, he uses words like "eclectic" to describe his taste in music (side note: should you ever want to reach out to me to discuss the strategies and techniques I used, especially for muscle tone, speech, and reading, please feel free to contact me at wendyhellowell@gmail.com).

And do you know what? Because everything was more difficult for him to achieve; because it took longer; because things proved to be more of a challenge; somehow, everything he did was so much more amazing. Everything was such a joy and a celebration, and NOTHING was taken for granted. EVERY step was simply WONDROUS!! My world and my life with Oliver has been SO much more vibrant and COLOURFUL than I could have ever imagined!!

All these years later, I can say to you with much confidence and with my whole heart, that I would never want to change who Oliver is. If someone gave me a magic wand that could take away him having Down syndrome, I would decline. Down Syndrome is woven into the very fabric of his being. If you took it away, he would no longer be the same Oliver. I love and adore him for exactly who he is, and I am so very proud of the son I have and who he's become. Some people may not agree with what I just wrote. Others might say something like, "But surely that is quite a selfish stance to take? Because if such a choice were possible, then surely you would want him to have a better life? As a person without Down syndrome, surely he would have a happier and more fulfilled life?"

Really though? My "abled" daughter Anna has significantly more worries, concerns, fears, obligations, responsibilities, and unhappiness in her life compared to Oliver. And as a parent, I worry more about Anna that I do Oliver. I challenge you to find an "ordinary" twenty year old who enjoys life as much as my son. He is never bored and has always been interested in so many things, even from a young age. He loves and has a keen eye for wildlife, nature, the countryside, animals, and birds (his knowledge and ability to identify any species of bird amazes me). He also loves skateboarding, football, snooker, and cars (he's a "Top Gear" fanatic and can identify any car you care to show him). Oliver is a history buff who loves to visit and explore castle ruins. He also has a passion for fishing and, of course, photography for which he is now quite well-known. He is hilarious and has a great sense of humour, even if it's a bit random at times! His unique perspective on life has taught me to view the world a little differently, and I am honestly a far better person for that.

Oh yes, I can't forget to mention connections. I'm not talking about electrical wires and junctions but about a meeting of souls, an unusual rare kind of reciprocity and a type of deep seated kinship. There is a special kind of affinity or closeness that develops between our children and those around them. Our children have an amazing ability to bring out the best in others. Oliver has amazing connections with several "special" people in his life. They are from all sorts of places and different parts of his life. They don't seem to have anything in common with Oliver other than their genuine and honest enjoyment of him for exactly who he is. They value him.

Throughout Oliver's life, I have found myself unfairly "judging" people who seem to react to our boy. I think as parents we develop an incredible type of parental "radar" or intuition where we assess and measure those around us. Others simply aren't fortunate enough to understand. On the flipside, because of Oliver, I have met the most valuable and important people in our lives. We have "collected" them along this wondrous journey and I am so deeply grateful for them.

By the way, in case you're wondering, Oliver's biological father left his life when he was about six years old. He was ignorant and chose to miss out on the golden connection that he could have had. Ultimately, he was not worthy of such an amazing son. As unfortunate as his leaving was, it was "meant to be" because Mike came into our world when Oliver was nine years old, and their connection was extraordinary and miraculous. I can assure you that Mike is Oliver's father in EVERY sense of the word now. At this point, I think I'll turn the storytelling over to Mike.

Mike's Entry

Hi there everyone. I'm Mike and I arrived in this community a little later than most of you. At the end of 2005, I found myself on my own and had made contact with an old friend, Wendy. We had seen each other briefly nine years earlier when Oliver had just returned home following heart surgery. Between that Christmas and New Year, I decided to drive up from Devon to Somerset to see Wendy and meet Oliver. When I met Oliver, we made an immediate and strong connection, which came as a surprise to both Wendy and myself. Over the next couple of years, I became increasingly more involved with Wendy, Oliver, and an amazing group of people who made me feel that I had found my place in life.

I am very aware that I wasn't there to experience those early years following the diagnosis, particularly all the accompanying fears and worries regarding Oliver's health and development. But I can honestly say that because of my involvement with Wendy, Oliver and the Down Syndrome community, and their collective acceptance of me, I have found a better part of myself. My life is so much more fulfilled and has a renewed purpose. I have been fortunate to take on new roles and have done the best I can. As Wendy noted earlier, I take great pride in being Oliver's father. I have laughed more than ever before and have discovered the greatest gifts available to us from our young people – raw honesty, pure joy, fun, mischief, humour (providing you accept the occasional random nature of it), and all with a huge smile!!

To finish my bit, I will tell you something Wendy told me early on – "Life around us may be challenging at times, but it will never be dull!!" Quite honestly folks, who on earth wants their life to be dull? And as I have said on a number of occasions, it's all about enjoying the madness!

And now, to follow Mike's words, here are a few words directly from Oliver. He is dictating as he is far too worried about writing in the precious book!! Oliver's words are as follows:

"Tell them not to worry about it, mum. I went to the awards for the UK, and I won! I was just like James Bond! I was a star! I've got Down syndrome and they said it was going to be difficult, but I find it easy. I've got Down syndrome but it's not the end of the world or anything. I was on TV on "The One Show" (BBC), and I loved it. I love my Dad, and my sister. I love my nieces too. Me and my sister like to go out. We have "brother-sister" days and I like them. Oh and my mother, well, she's awesome...most of the time."

Oliver is fortunate enough to have an extended family through Mike. Aside from Mike, Anna, and myself, Oliver has a step-sister, two step-brothers, and several nieces and nephews. These "extra" family members are extremely important to Oliver, and he in turn is valued and loved by them. His relationship with his two nieces is particularly strong and so incredibly touching to witness.

I have a dear friend named Kareen, who I supported when her son was born with Down syndrome and again as they dealt with various traumatic cardiac surgeries. Her son Jack is now sixteen years old, and she says the following about him: "Waking up to this boy every morning is similar to the feeling you had as a child when you realized it was the first day of the summer holidays." I am also fortunate enough to know the amazing Critchlow family whose daughter Emily (who is now in her twenties) recently said, "Down syndrome has been spectacular for me!"

And so, dear reader, here we are today. If I was to offer you only one piece of advice, it would be to ENJOY your child and EVERY MOMENT with him or her. In the beginning, I know it's difficult to imagine, but honestly, it is SO IMPORTANT. Enjoy the difference he or she brings to your life! I wanted to tell you these stories because no one was able to tell me anything positive when Oliver was born and diagnosed. I simply sat weeping on my own in that little hospital room holding my baby. But looking back on our life together, Oliver completely lights up my every day. He makes us laugh and look at the world differently, and I am eternally blessed and grateful for that. He loves his friends and family, and he is dearly loved, enjoyed and valued by them. Oliver is a wonderful, hilarious, talented, extraordinary, random, awesome young man! And this world is more vibrant and richer with him in it!

Note: Oliver has a Facebook page for his photography with a following of over 65,000 people and through his website, we receive orders for his prints from all over the world. Last year, he published the first-ever book of photography by a person with Down syndrome. Since the initial writing of this entry, Oliver has published two more books and was commissioned by the Tennessee Board of Tourism to capture the beauty of Smoky Mountains National Park in his own unique way. A short film was made about the journey (by Simon Weitzman). During this time, Oliver met an internationally renowned local photographer called Ken Jenkins, and the two bonded over breakfast and bacon, and discussions about local birdlife. The connection between them was instant and despite living across the world from each other, they have maintained an extraordinary relationship.

www.facebook.com/OliverHellowellPhotographer

www.oliverhellowell.com

And do you know what?

Because everything was more difficult for him to achieve, because it took longer, because things proved to be more of a challenge - somehow - that just made everything he did so much more amazing. It was always such a joy and celebration. NOTHING was taken for granted and so EVERY step was WONDROUS!!

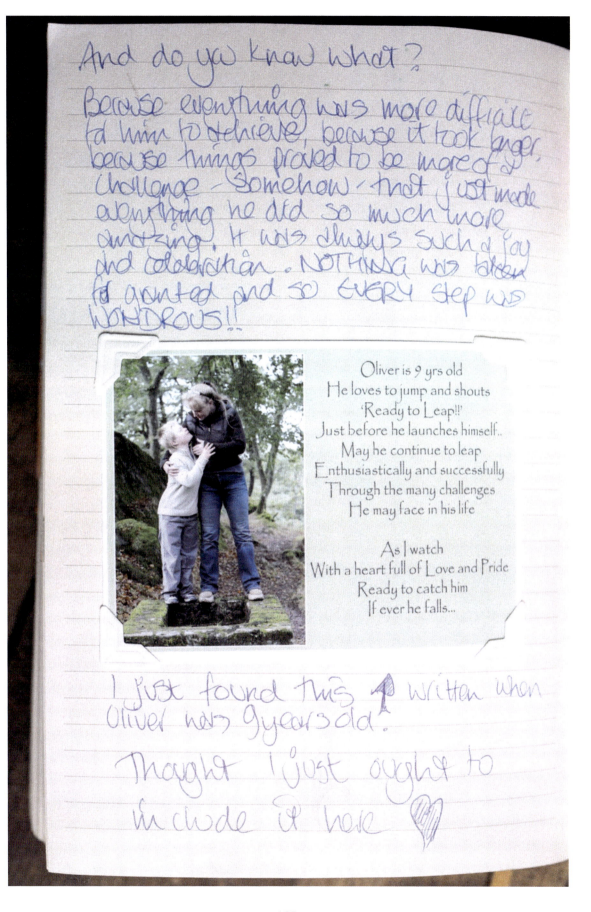

Oliver is 9 yrs old
He loves to jump and shouts
'Ready to Leap!!'
Just before he launches himself..
May he continue to leap
Enthusiastically and successfully
Through the many challenges
He may face in his life

As I watch
With a heart full of Love and Pride
Ready to catch him
If ever he falls...

I just found this ↑ written when Oliver was 9 years old!

Thought I just ought to include it here

Oliver is fortunate enough to have
family through Mike - as well

Enjoy Every moment!

Hayley & Natty

"It seems that we are intrinsically driven to change the world from within. Because it counts. It's personal. We do it for our children. This diary is binding proof of that."

—Hayley Newman

Natalia Hope Goleniowska
Born on 6th/December 2006 at home

A sister for Mia Amber
Daughter to Hayley

Down's Syndrome was identified at around 6 hours old.

Cornwall, UK

Blog: www.downssideup.com
Twitter/Insta/FB @DownsSideUp
Books: I Love You Natty
       Talking About Down's Syndrome

nd so it arrived…

A book that feels as precious as a historic scroll. You know, the sort you see on TV where the presenter has to wear gloves before they can even touch it.

That's how The Down Syndrome Diary feels to me. Maybe it's the hand-scribed messages inside an aged leather binding. Or the countless hours that so many families have lovingly poured their hearts and souls into it. Perhaps it's the occasional tear stain on a book that has taken over three years to reach our home from its start point.

I must admit to welling up when I opened the package, complete with a gift and message of love from the family who went before us. We opened it live on Facebook and watchers felt the raw emotion. This, 1st in a series of diaries inching its way around the world, is real and personal, being passed from hand to hand in the manner of traditional story-telling, rather than relying on 2 dimensional digital shares.

"We know what we are, but know not what we may be."

—Shakespere

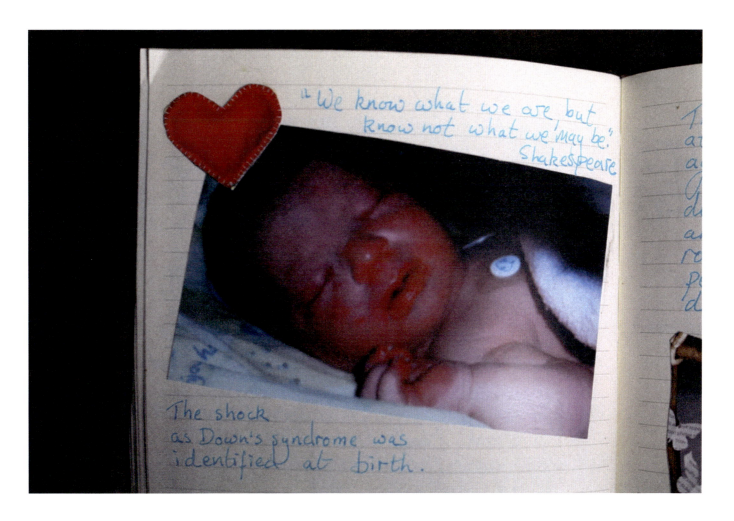

As the time came to write here, I felt so in awe of the power within the pages. I found myself holding back, afraid to mark the paper with ink. Just as when Natty was born, I felt uncertain and unable to find the words to describe my emotions.

As I read through the previous stories, I knew at once that everything I can tell you about our journey had already been told.

The shared experiences of shock at an unexpected diagnosis, the agonising fear as our child's fate lay in the hands of a stranger during heart surgery. The pride, love, and deep desire to shout from the rooftops that our families are perfect and complete, were already detailed in full.

Others have told you of the wonderful, unpredictable, hurly burly of our lives. They've described their offsprings' incredible talents, their strength, sharp sense of humour, many achievements, and perfect everyday ordinariness.

We've also seen that despite our initial fears, the brothers and sisters grow up considerate, passionate, and fair.

So I wrote her this poem:

To Natty
I love you so much
and you are the best sister in the world
and so precious to me.

You are so important to me
and if you weren't in this world
my life wouldn't be the same
and that wouldn't be fun.

So, I love you very very
much and you mean
everything to me…

I wrote this when I was 9 so obviously my perspective has changed a bit now. I still love her though!

Mia

So I wrote her this poem:

To Natty
I love you so much
and you are the best sister in the world
and so precious to me.

You are so important to me
and if you weren't in this world
my life wouldn't be the same
and that wouldn't be fun.

So, I love you very very
much and you mean
everything to me..

I wrote this
when I was 9
so obviously my
perspective has changed a bit now.
I still love her though!

Mia

Our story contains differences in detail of course, a gentle home birth, a doula's care, support-ive friends, medical angels who uplifted us, and others whose words caused pain.

There's been modelling, stealing cake on live TV, national newspaper articles, a Lord Mayor of London's fancy dress party, lots of celebs, tea with the Queen and a book. This all breaks down barriers, but what really matters is that both our girls know they are unique and special and loved just as they are.

Reading through others' accounts I see that it isn't just the emotions that we have in com-mon. There are so many award-winning blogs and books written, billboards adorned, support groups, and charities started and world firsts of all kinds.

It seems that we are intrinsically driven to change the world from within. Because it counts. It's personal. We do it for our children. This diary is binding proof of that.

Families like ours have always campaigned for equitable, quality healthcare, rights to education, and respect for our children who are the true trailblazers.

Together, we are constantly pushing limits, challenging wrongs, and paying support forward to those starting out on the path behind us.

So for me, the diary symbolises our international family, our exclusive club that spans race, religion, age, and socio political background. The community I wanted to avoid with all my heart until I found myself thrust into it. Here I found my safety net and the warmest, dearest friends. Our children are truly the greatest ice-breakers, and Down syndrome a fantastic leveller.

Welcomed by families in Mauritius

And just as I was wrong about not wanting to be in 'The Special Needs Club' I was wrong to think we'd never travel again after Natty was born. Despite living ten minutes from the sea, I feared our feet would never again walk on sand.

My mind was creating borders for our daughter. Stereotypes and fears led to imaginings of people pointing, staring, and laughing.

Of course, the reverse is true and, like the diary we have travelled far and wide as a family. It takes planning and patience, but Natty breaks the ice in every new location.

On a journey...

And just as I was wrong about being in 'The Special Needs Club' I was wrong to think we'd never travel again after Natty was born. Despite living ten minutes from the sea, I feared our feet would never again walk on sand.

Just as this book fills out and develops, we all as young people with Down's syndrome, parents, grandparents, siblings, and teachers are on a learning curve together. We gather anecdotes, pictures and wisdoms, none of us knowing what obstacle or change of path is around the corner.

But, as dear old Dr. Seuss would say,

"Oh, the places you'll go!"

Just as this book fills out and develops, we all, as parents, grandparents, siblings and teachers are on a learning curve.
We gather anecdotes, pictures and wisdoms, none of us knowing what obstacle or change of path is around the corner.

But, as dear old Dr. Seuss would say,

"Oh, the places you'll go!"

Hey, it's Mia. Natty's sister.

When I wrote the book I was 9. My 13th birthday is in 3 days and there's a big age gap there. In the poem everything is true but what I forgot to mention is that life is not always perfect like that. Natty is the best sister in the whole world but there are definitely some occasions when I'm tired or in a bad mood and Natty gets on my nerves a bit. But that's totally normal. Don't all siblings annoy each other sometimes?! Isn't that what the whole point of having a brother or sister in the first place!

The point is that yes brothers and sisters are annoying, but I just want to tell everyone to be proud of your siblings, give them confidence and always believe in them because I know that if my sister says she wants to do something, she will make it her mission to do that thing.

Always
    Believe
        In
            Your
                Siblings!
Because if you do...they will achieve!

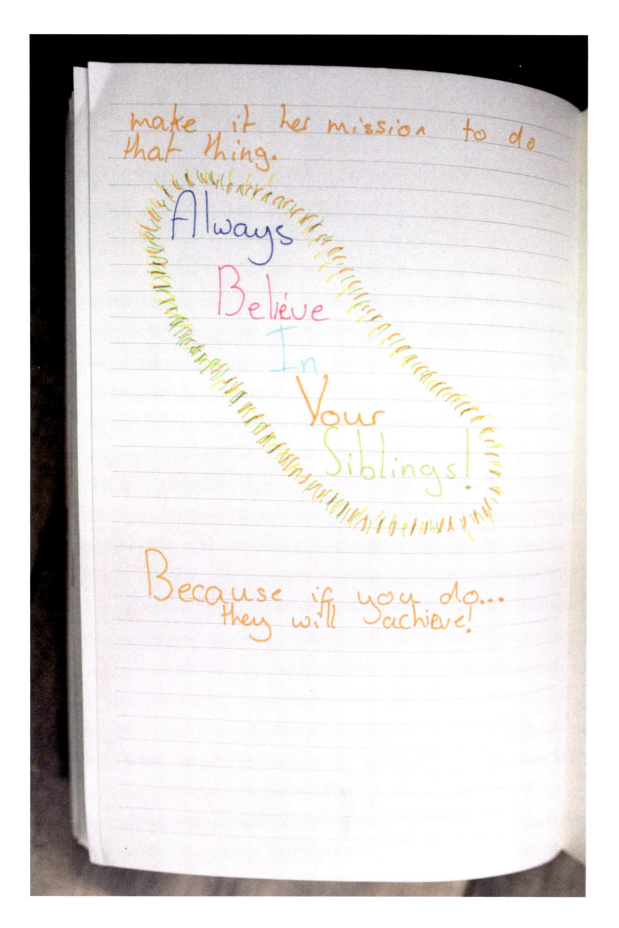

make it her mission to do that thing.

Always
Believe
In
Your
Siblings!

Because if you do...
they will achieve!

Wyn & Angharad

Nikki, Wyn & Angharad

"There is not one thing I'd change about her. I just hope that Nikki and I will be around for a long time yet so that we can watch with pride as she continues to change the world around her!"

—Wyn Evans

Angharad Catrin Evans
Cardiff, Wales, UK

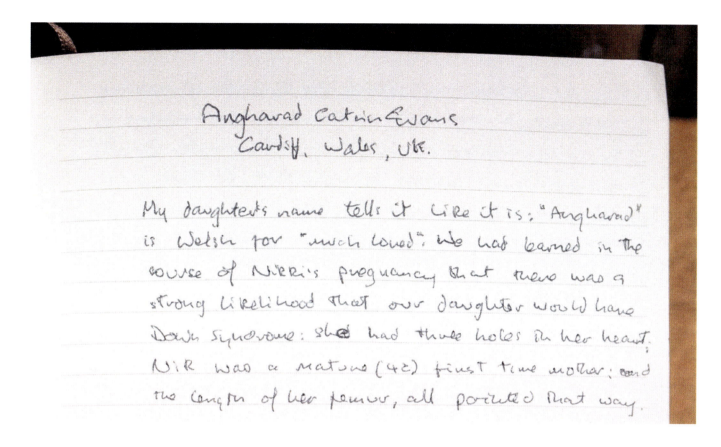

My daughter's name tells it like it is: "Angharad" is Welsh for "much loved." We had learned in the course of Nikki's pregnancy that there was a strong likelihood that our daughter would have Down Syndrome (DS): at 42, Nik was a mature first time mother; scans showed our baby had three holes in her heart; and the length of the femur, all pointed that way.

Angharad was born on a Tuesday and her extra chromosome was not identified until the Friday following. Throughout the pregnancy, midwives and doctors had pointed out to us what they called the 'necessity' of having an amniocentesis and stressed the availability of abortion. They did this despite Nikki repeatedly asking for her medical notes to highlight that she would *not* be seeking an amnio and would *not* be having a termination of her pregnancy.

When the doctor told us that Friday that our daughter had DS it was with a sad voice and a long face. We had a little cry – it seemed expected and finally knowing for certain was definitely a release of pressure.

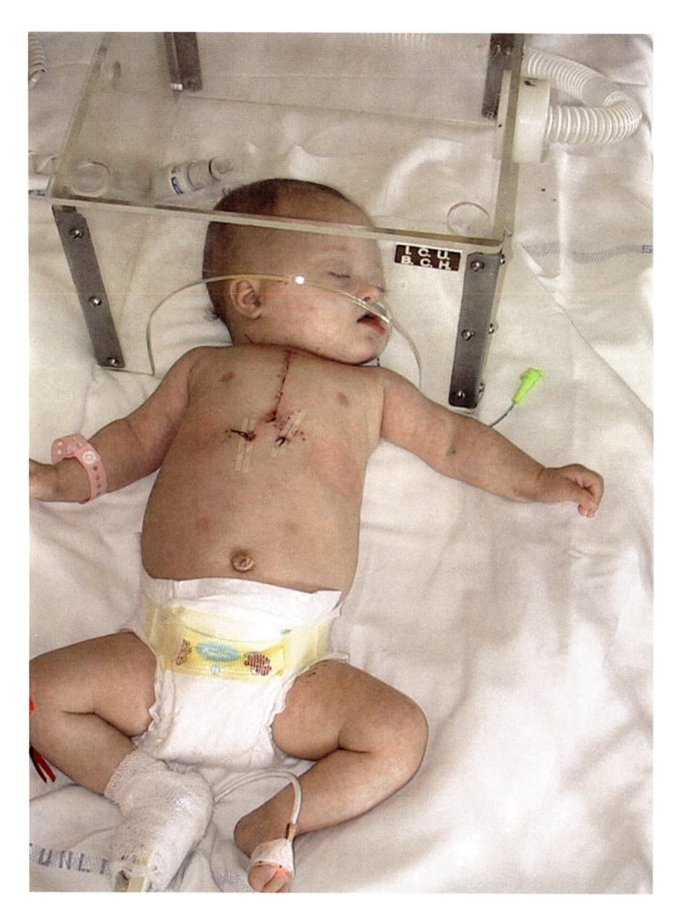

Angharad (or Ace) was born five weeks prematurely. She weighed 3lbs 10oz, could fit in the palm of my hand, and spent her first six weeks in ICU. She required open heart surgery, which she was able to have aged 15 weeks. Post operation, when she was well enough to be with us in our hospital room, she scared us by making her first ever scream. We jumped in fright! It was explained to us that before the holes in her heart were fixed she hadn't had enough energy or strength to make much noise. I'd never before realised what a life-affirming thing a baby's cry could be.

Despite issues with feeding, with hypotonia, with needing to use Makaton sign language (which was a godsend) and despite some people's attitudes being in the Dark Ages, we were determined that Ace would be a part of and contribute to the local community of which we were (are) a part; we joined every activity and group imaginable.

Nikki took a year's maternity leave then returned to work as the breadwinner. I left my job and became a full-time dad. At coffee mornings, baby massage, swimming, singing, and other activities I was generally warmly welcomed by the other parents who were mostly mums (or mams as we say here in Wales!). We tried to give Angharad as many different peer groups as possible: mainstream/typically developing kids, kids with DS, kids with other disabilities, etc.

We found a pre-school nursery that welcomed Ace with open arms. Her low-tone meant that she found some activities difficult but she bounced and rolled and eventually walked her way into a local primary school. In both nursery and in reception class she had 1:1 support that primarily focused on Speech Therapy. When the National Health Service/Local Education Authority speech therapy provision dried-up or was simply over-stretched, we paid for private provision – an hour a week, every week – which is still ongoing. (Ace is now nearly fifteen years of age and is in her fourth year of High school.) As an aside, Nik and I believe that learning Makaton and accessing good S&L therapy have been the two most helpful interventions we facilitated for Ace.

During Angharad's primary schooling she attended a Specialist Resource Base (SRB) each morning and then joined her typically-developing peers for afternoon lessons. This model worked well, on the whole, for all concerned. However, we believed that Ace would gain more (and give more back) if she could attend a mainstream High school without an SRB but with 1:1 support and a curriculum differentiated for her capabilities. We started discussions with Cardiff High School well in advance and were heartened by staff's preparedness to make this happen. Thus, Ace is the first child with DS ever to attend Cardiff High School. It matters in all sorts of ways but it is especially significant for us as it is Angharad's local comprehensive school and serves all the kids in this community. We have now started investigating Ace's educational options for her post-sixteen years.

Her activities? Angharad climbs Boulders' rock-faces, rides horses through trotting and cantering, is readying for her fourth judo belt (put on hold because of the pandemic lockdown), and has lessons at a local swimming club. She has loved every minute of Rainbows and Brownies and is now a Girl Guide Ranger. Her two "most favourite" activities are ballet and trampolining. She holds her own with her typically-developing peers in ballet gradings (currently grade six); has been runner-up in her category in the British Trampolining Championships, also representing Wales in trampolining. She attends a local youth group for kids who have Down syndrome and this gives her great happiness. Most recently she has signed-up for weekly singing lessons.

I can't be doing with those people who think having a child diagnosed with DS is the end of the world as they know it. Sorry if that was you, dear reader! Nik and I are not "pushy parents," we just believe in our daughter to do as well as she can at whatever she turns her hand to. Our job is to love and protect her and facilitate her development. We expect her to be further educated. We expect she will pass her driving test if she decides she wants to do so. She tells us that one day she wants to have an interesting job and to settle down and have a family and we'll do all we can to support her if, in due course, this happens.

Don't get me started on health and social policy makers who are trying to eradicate DS from the world as if it was akin to malaria. "Non-Invasive

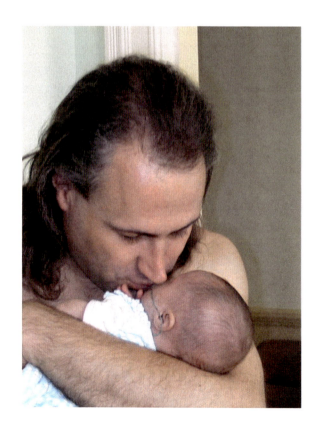

Prenatal Testing (NIPT)," while potentially a useful tool in helping prepare families for all eventualities, risks instead being used with abortion to prevent the birth of future generations of people with DS. We are nonetheless heartened by the bottom-up, family-driven work that advocates for those with DS. This has seen the development of helpful and positive information for would-be parents of kids with DS. It has seen changes to the curriculums of doctors, nurses, and midwives in training – so that they actually meet and are lectured-to by people with DS and their families.

Surveys show that most people with DS are really happy with their lives. Families and friends of those with DS know what they bring to the party. **Now** is the best time ever to be a person who has DS, or to be a parent, sibling or friend of someone with DS:

- Surgical and pharmaceutical interventions are adding years to life and life to years, extending mean life expectancy into the sixties, which will certainly continue to rise;
- Speech and other therapies mean that people with DS can be understood and can play their part in the babble that is our daily life.
- Educationalists know more about how best to tailor programmes of education to the needs and learning styles of those with DS.
- There are plenty of examples of how to tailor the employment and housing markets to give those with DS real opportunities for employment and independence.

Angharad has featured in our local and national press and on broadcast media. I have written a monthly magazine column about her for eight years; this has opened up many interesting opportunities for dialogue and mutual education with members of the public. My Facebook blog with 77,000 followers. All these things suggest that there is a well of goodwill out there. It is important to see all the things that people with DS *can* do rather than be overwhelmed by things that they cannot.

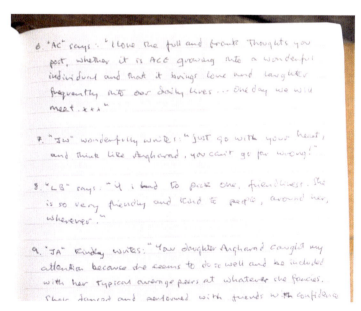

With this Down Syndrome Diary entry in mind, I asked a few people to let me know what reading about Angharad has done for their lives. Here are a few of the comments that they sent me:

- "KC" writes, "Angharad has shown us that joining in mainstream activities isn't only possible but it is also successful. Having met Angharad, we have loved the clarity of her speech."
- "LF" notes, "For me it is the journal of not just a child but of a family. Your family has its own struggles, just as mine does, and it is the reality of life with DS mixed in with these struggles that makes it real."
- "SJ" writes, "For me… the one thing that always makes me smile, and reminds me of my late mum, is that you instill into Angharad the mantra 'there's no such word as 'can't.'' This in itself sets up a self-belief and confidence that she'll take with her into adulthood."
- "JF" says, "Your blog has introduced me to the wider D.S. community and a whole range of information sources which have been a huge help, but it has been wonderful to gain friends – other parents dealing with the same hurdles and concerns. It is wonderful to be able to share in our family life and Ace inspires me to ensure that we give (our daughter) as many opportunities to embrace and pursue her passions in life. Thank You."
- "LO" notes, "The most poignant part of Angharad's nature is her caring side… Ace is very open with emotions and will show her feelings, which is truly endearing… she's not afraid to speak her mind, which is refreshing too! You know where you stand, there is no facade, just pure truth and openness, which is what we all really want to hear… last time I saw Ace I asked for a cuddle. She agreed but said "it has to be quick." You can't get more honest than that! It's a joy to be around her. Don't ever change Ace, because you are beautiful on the inside and outside. xxx."
- "AC" says, "I love the full and frank thoughts you post, whether it is Ace growing into a wonderful individual and that it brings love and laughter frequently into our daily lives… one day we will meet. xxx"
- "JW" wonderfully writes, "Just go with your heart, and think like Angharad, you can't go far wrong!"
- "LB" says, "If I had to pick one, friendliness. She is so very friendly and kind to people around her, whenever."
- "JA" kindly writes, "Your daughter Angharad caught my attention because she seems to do so well and be included with her typical average peers at whatever she fancies. She's danced and performed with friends with confidence and joy. It doesn't appear that she was pulled into an activity to occupy her time. Ace seems to truly find joy in that activity. You and Nikki have created a normal world for her with school, family, and friends. I was very interested to learn about Ace's speech ability to express herself. As you know, DS hinders many people from connecting with others, even with their families. My little one turned seven years old a few months ago and struggles to talk. My girl is frustrated as

a result. I wanted to know if there was hope for us to find role-models. Angharad has been that for my family. She is a model of what is possible with perseverance, support, and faith. We love her life story here in Texas."

- "SB" says, "I'm struck by how 'free' pics of her feel."

Just a few comments there from people who have been positively influenced by Angharad. There is not one thing I'd change about her. I just hope that Nikki and I will be around for a long time yet so that we can watch with pride as she continues to change the world around her!

(You can follow Angharad at: https://www.facebook.com/BeatingDownsBarriers/)

Megan, Erik, & Millie

"Down syndrome was never the end of our story, it was
the cliffhanger right before the real story began."

—Megan Fortman

Megan Fortman
Tecumseh, MI USA

Written 3/15/18

Amelia is going to be a big sister this year. While I knew I would experience worry, I really didn't expect this new pregnancy to tear open the old wound that was a birth diagnosis. When Amelia was born unexpectedly with Down syndrome, we felt completely helpless and unprepared for the baby looking back at us. We felt alone, isolated and terrified to tell even each other how we were really feeling. Sadness followed by guilt played on repeat in my head and heart. I felt stripped of everything I thought I knew and stuck on a mary-go-round that I so badly wanted to jump off of, never looking back.

I didn't want this baby to change what felt like an almost perfect life. I thought she would slow us down or keep us from the fulfilling life I had always dreamt of. I thought she would have no personality or interests and be a burden to her siblings. I didn't know a single person with Down syndrome and couldn't help but think our "luck" had run out. I had two beautiful, healthy children already, why did I push for a third? Oh how wrong I was.

When I first learned of the "Down Syndrome Diary", I was sitting in our hospital bed staring at my three day old baby. She was happily swaddled like a little burrito on my lap. She had a cannula in her nose and two strips of medical tape on her perfectly round cheeks. It's funny to think at the time I didnt even know what a cannula was called and now thanks to Amelia I'm a wealth of random medical knowledge! I was frantically scouring social media for families that might look like mine who could provide some

insight and maybe even hope. My eyes were swollen, I had had a non stop headache from all of the crying and I felt like one giant, raw wound. I didn't want to know what the medical world had to say about my baby and her diagnosis. I wanted to talk to Moms like me. I wanted to see Daddies snuggling their baby girls, big brothers picking on them and big sisters putting on their makeup. Our birth story seemed like a very personal nightmare. Karma perhaps for any and all wrong doing I had ever done. Where did we fit? Who is safe? Who are our people now? I saw a link for the diary online and after a few minutes realized this community was created for people who felt exactly like I did. With one simple "Hi I'm new here" email, I was connected to a whole new world. Little did I know at the time this new world would hold not only my very best friends but also my entire life's purpose.

The support from my new tribe was immediate and I was flooded with emails from parents CONGRATULATING me and pouring out words of encouragement and advice. Had you told me in three short months from then I would be the head over heels in love Mom proudly emailing an obnoxious amount of photos of my baby girl to new parents, I wouldn't have believed you. I never expected "advocate" to be my favorite title, directly behind Momma and wife.

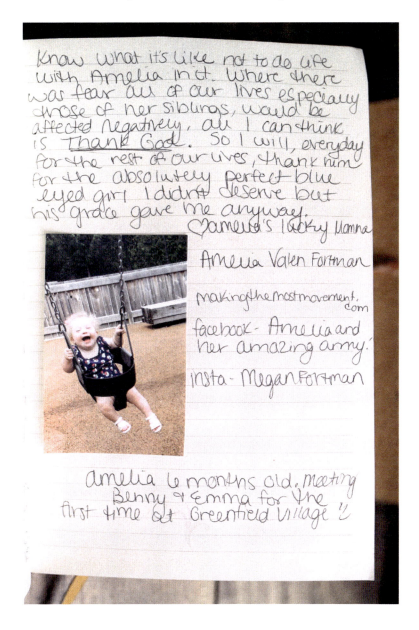

I describe Down syndrome like a healthy marriage. There are times when it is a lot of work. The journey changes and looks different all of the time but the pay off of spending your life with your best friend makes every hill worth climbing. MOST days being Amelia's Mom looks extremely typical. Other days being a Mom to a child with extraordinary needs is different and even hard but I learned pretty quickly that those days are the very ticket we didn't know we needed, to the most meaningful life. The ticket that brought us all here together. The ticket that truly makes us the Lucky Ones. The beautiful reminder that the best version of ourselves lives on the outside of our comfort zone, along with our greatest gifts.

Had the choice been mine to make, chances are I wouldn't have chosen this life. I wouldn't have thought I could handle it. I would have missed this opportunity. I have never felt so at home or purposeful since becoming Millie's Mom. I belong here, where the sun always shines and the silver lining is always bright. Where any bad day can be turned around with one smile from a girl who is my world. We are kinder, stronger, more compassionate humans because of her. Without Amela I wouldn't have found my voice or the gratitude well that never runs dry. I would have missed her big sister Brooklynn becoming an advocate or her big brother Gable teaching her sign language and the way they adore her. I would have missed watching the biggest Daddy's girl on the planet laugh at all of his jokes.I would have missed the bear hugs from a girl who knows nothing but whole hearted, genuine love.

Down syndrome was never the end of our story, it was the cliffhanger right before the real story began. My best advice for new parents is to take it one day at a time. Don't let the fear of tomorrow rob you of the newborn baby who wants nothing more than to melt into your arms. Follow their lead. People with Down syndrome are truly warriors with unmatched strength and tenacity. Don't ever underestimate their power or purpose and enjoy your gift from God. Amelia is truly an angel on earth and I still can't believe I get to call her mine.

Love,

Amelia's lucky Momma

2021 Update:

Today Amelia is almost seven years old and I can proudly announce she dominated becoming a big sister. She participates in dance, soccer, pre-k, is writing most of the letters in her name and can shoot hoops with ease. She's made amazing relationships, flourished and continues to smash milestones. Disney's Elsa, her family, ice cream and yelling "BOOTYCHEEKS!" are her favorite things. The sense of independence she gained at school catapulted her into the sassy, doesn't take no for an answer Millie V she is today. Amelia is an amazing big sister and a pest as a little one. She is the silliest daughter, full of pranks and jokes and the sweetest granddaughter. She loves with her entire being.. She is an absolute force to be reckoned with and is the most motivated person I know. She is a people magnet and our little local celebrity. Amelia is not at all the person I thought she would be and so much more than I could have ever hoped for.

Amelia Valen Fortman
Makingthemostmovement.com
Facebook – Amelia & Her Amazing Army
Instagram – Megan Fortman

Amelia's Dad
Written 3-22-18

Erik Fortman
Tecumseh, MI,USA
Instagram: @Erikfortman

Thrice in my life I have met someone who made me change my entire life, but just once have I met someone who made me want to change the world.

Dear New Down Syndrome Dad,

You're sitting there in your hospital chair trying to figure out whether to pull your hair out or watch it as it slowly turns white right before your puffy and red swollen eyes. You feel so alone, so scared, and scared that you're now forever alone.

You won't be for long. Soon you'll have more love in your heart than you ever knew was possible.

Pull your hair out or watch it as it slowly turns white right before your eyes... Feeling so alone. And scared. And scared that now you're forever alone.

You won't be... Soon you'll have more love in your heart then you ever knew was possible.

I know you... The dad sitting there in the hospital chair, or just standing there taking a break between your restless and endless pacing

I know you well. The dad sitting in the hospital chair taking a break between your restless and endless pacing. Ready to tackle every book you can, and soak up all the new terminology being thrown at you from every direction.

Don't do that, not yet anyway. You have plenty of time to learn. If you do it now you will only scare yourself and miss this very special moment.

Like I said, I know you...

You are scared. Scared to look at that baby...You're scared to look at your phone or check social media. You know that if you do that it will become real. That this nightmare you never imagined will become your new reality. But it is! And here it is right in front of you! Looking you right in the eyes. It is very real. It is the single most real thing that has ever happened in your entire life.

You're forgetting something. This is not about you, not at all.

Am I hitting the nail on the head? If not I'll bet I'm pretty close. Close to home, and close to your heart.

I Know all this because I was you. Not very long ago I was the dad in the hospital chair, with the sad and swollen eyes trying to decide whether to pull my hair out or watch it slowly turn white. I thought my life as I knew it was over. That it would never be the same again. And I was right! The life I live now is nothing like I ever imagined.

When Amelia (Millie) was born I just kept thinking "God gives his biggest battles to his toughest soldiers" and I was ready to take on all of those tough battles myself. I quickly realized that was true, but that soldier wasn't me, it was her... Amelia was that soldier, and to this day it's always been true. She has taken on and conquered everything that has been put in front of her and done it with a smile. The littlest and most innocent person I know is also the most impactful and powerful person in my life. I've watched her change her siblings and our entire extended family, the way we live, the way we see the world, the words we use and the way we love. I've seen her change not only our small town but enhance the lives of an entire community. She brings out the best in every person she meets.She never misses a chance to greet a stranger, or share a smile. The ray of light from her soul encompasses every room she enters and makes it a better kinder place.

From the bottom of my heart, congrats Dad. You have just been blessed with the greatest gift of all. Enjoy this ride, and don't miss another minute worrying about anything. There will be ups and downs along the way just like everything in this life. But the love is more profound, the sweetness is more rich, the hugs are tighter,and the milestones are greater. One day you will look back upon this day and realize this is it. This is when your next chapter truly began.

Amelia's lucky dad,

Erik Fortman

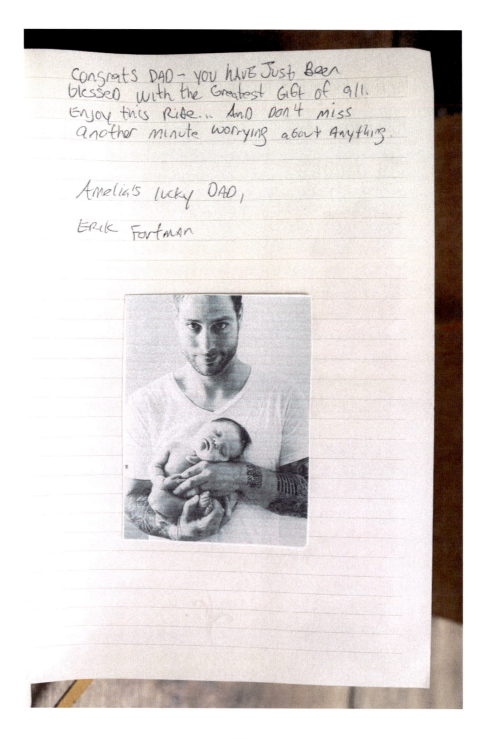

Victoria & Audrey

"At the time this all seemed so huge, so unfair, but now I just look back on it like a small blip, I guess we've just come so far."

—Vicky Baynton-Williams

Vicky Baynton-Williams
Hove, East Sussex, UK

Written: 10th April 2018

My daughter is Audrey, born 22nd July 2013.

This week, I was pushing Audrey along in the buggy with her younger brother (Rex), when my thoughts drifted, and I started to cry. Audrey's emotional intelligence is impressive to say the least, and she turned to me, offering her tiny hand and asked, "Mummy? Are you ok Mummy?" I held her hand and reassured her because, yes, I was ok. I was actually crying with joy.

It was a culmination of thoughts – firstly several (very common) incidents of people commenting on Audrey's kind nature. "If only more people were like her…"/ "Your daughter is so kind, she was bringing toys over to my baby"/"Audrey was very kind and gave up the toys she was playing with so my child would stop having a tantrum"/"She's so friendly and confident"/ "I know I shouldn't say this, but your daughter is my favorite."

Secondly a friend mentioning that she had started to remember having a best friend at primary school with Down's syndrome...How she made her laugh, the play dates they had at her big house.

And lastly, Audrey's 1:1 keyworker at nursery, expressing that she would like to follow Audrey into primary school as her 1:1 assistant there.

I realised reasonably quickly after Audrey's diagnosis that we, as her family, would love her, but I never anticipated how many other people would love her too. In fact, I think (know) I feared that people wouldn't love her – that we might be actively avoided! How wrong I was.

We found out Audrey had Down's syndrome after she was born. After a happy relaxed pregnancy, I went into hospital a few days after our due date, when I realised Audrey wasn't moving. So very quickly, from no labour to monitoring to emergency C-section – we had a baby. My husband held her first, wrapped in a towel, and I caught a glimpse of her face. I saw "it" immediately. <u>Down's syndrome.</u> I remember asking him to show me more of her face. She had lots of ginger hair, and I said she looked like a monkey! As soon as she was placed on my chest for skin to skin, I saw nothing but Down's syndrome, and I remember my exact words (to my husband), "<u>This baby</u> has Down's syndrome."

Audrey had a little trouble breathing at first, so we stayed in the hospital – She spent the first 3 weeks of her life in the special care baby unit and remained on oxygen when she came home for 6 months. At the time this all seemed so huge, so unfair, but now I just look back on it like a small blip, I guess we've just come so far.

My husband always says he remembers that moment when Audrey and I bonded. When he could see we would all "be ok" – It was when, less than a day old, I held her and she started to breastfeed. I looked up and with pride, exclaimed, "She's doing it!" And that's just how things have gone.

Audrey gives us a reason to be proud everyday. She turns 5 next month and starts school this year, yet it feels like only yesterday she was bottom shuffling around with little interest in walking! And you know, it's not great to have a 2 year old that can't run around with her friends – but somehow it was ok. Somehow we got through and now she's got a younger brother to chase around!

The biggest "hurdle" if you like was the change in path. The lost expectations. I'm actually really surprised by how much I had already pictured of my "future daughter." The shopping trips we'd have, the clothes we'd share (sounds a bit hopeful, but I shared clothes with my mother!!) What job one might have, etc. That projection seems crazy to me now. Especially as my husband and I are very open and liberal people. We are trying to ensure we raise well-rounded humans who believe in equality and I guess part of the early "grieving process" was partly being upset with myself – I wasn't quite so open-minded as I had thought! I couldn't see Audrey as Audrey – I only saw a condition and that scared me. And I'm not saying that's gone away – I get scared still, mostly by the world around her and how she might be treated by others, but in terms of Audrey as a person and her future – well I'm excited! Truly excited to see how she progresses and what she will achieve. She is going to a mainstream school, and I know that as much as she has to learn, she has the same amount to teach others.

It's incredibly cheesy to say this (but I'm going to!): we have been on an incredible journey. Had I received this diary at a different time, I know my entry could be much more emotional and my "birth story" would have been pages and pages. It took me a while to not keep revisiting Audrey's birth – It was a bruise I liked to poke, to feel the pain again and again, punishing myself for the dark, negative feelings. But now I appreciate that time – That we've come such a long way and that if I could return to that scared new mother, in desperate mourning for her "perfect" baby – I would have so much to say! Most importantly, so much to show – everything Audrey has achieved from her Makaton signing, fabulous speech progression, how she can sing (from "The Wheels on the Bus" to Katy Perry's "Roar"), she dances like no one is watching.

...ums and my heart swells
...de.
...ntly had a
... job and
...sure how it
... - the fear
...often creeps
...there. I
..."special
...abel dress)
...will it be
...her? Will
...se to wear
...ves? Yet
...he totally
...d me by
...eing totally
...l. Easy-
...lots of fun,
...d. She was
...lete pro!!
...o, life with Audrey is
...y and everything like I
...equired!! Such is life.

She greets a room of strangers like they are her best friends, and she lights up the world with her personality. There is no question that our lives are better for having Audrey in it. Every challenge has made the outcome that bit sweeter – learning to walk took a lot of hard work and determination (on all our parts – I cried many tears helping Audrey with physiotherapy), sometimes I worry/doubt she can do something, like climbing difficult ladders in playgrounds – so often she ends up proving my wrong and she is always so proud of herself for overcoming a challenge. "I'm doing it for myself!" She exclaims and my heart swells with pride. She recently had a modelling job, and I wasn't sure how it might go – the fear that so often creeps in – was there. I let the "special needs" label stress me out. Will it be noisy for her? Will she refuse to wear the clothes? Yet again, she totally surprised me by being totally wonderful. Easy-going, lots of fun, relaxed. She was a complete pro!! And so, life with Audrey is nothing and everything like I imagined!! Such is life. How can you ever know what your child might be like? Why do we project so far? All you ever may need to know is that your child will hold your heart in their tiny hand and you will love them with such fearsome force.

You will do all you can to fight for their rights and will babble on in actual pen on actual paper to make sure people know this!!

– Vicky

2021 Update:

Re-reading this was fun. It was better than I remembered. Audrey turns eight this year and has been in mainstream school for nearly three years, she has come such a long way... still singing Katy Perry's "Roar" regularly though! The older she gets, the more excited I become for my future with grown up Audrey, that daughter I always dreamed about is here now: my best friend and the most empathetic human I know. She's also hilarious, stubborn, and wakes up too early, but to reiterate all I've said time and time again: I wouldn't change her.

Love them with such fearsome force, you will do all you can to fight for their rights and will dabble on in actual pen on actual paper to make sure people know this!! x

Mark, Karena, Eve & Dan

"From that point, I was determined that Dan would be given a fair shot at living, wearing cool clothes, rocking out to cool music, and changing the image of DS."

—Mark Jones

Mark, Karena, Eve & Dan

Karena Jones
Mark Jones
Eve Jones

Forest of Dean – Gloucestershire, UK
22nd August 2018

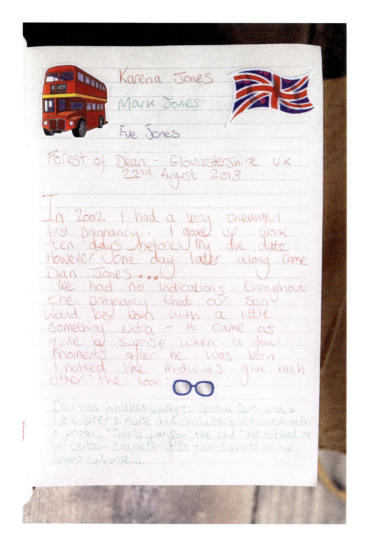

Karena:

In 2002, I had a very uneventful first pregnancy. I gave up work ten days before my due date, however just one day later along came Dan Jones.

We had no indications throughout the pregnancy that our son would be born with a little something "extra." It came as quite a surprise when a few moments after he was born I noticed the midwives gave each other "the look."

Mark:

Dan was whisked away to special care, and a little later a nurse and consultant returned with a photo. "This is your son," she said. "We noticed he has certain characteristics that support he has Down's Syndrome."

I remember it was announced to us quite somberly, like the end of the world had arrived. All I could think about was the long term future. Where will he be schooled? What will everyone's expectations be?

Karena:

In those first moments, it was all a bit overwhelming. My initial thoughts make me cringe now. Would he be that character from our childhood? Memories of the 1980's people with Down's

Syndrome with a bad haircut, overweight with ill fitting clothes – NO WAY! This is DAPPER DAN we are talking about!

Mark:

From that point, I was determined that Dan would be given a fair shot at living, wearing cool clothes, rocking out to cool music, and changing the image of DS.

Alongside the DS diagnosis, it was also announced that he had an imperforate anus. This meant his lower intestine stopped a little short of where it should, and would require immediate surgery to begin correcting it.

Karena:

In total, Dan required a series of three operations to correct his bowel condition. Unfortunately, he has never gained full control and requires daily catheterisation (but this is better than the colostomy bag he had before). We have been doing this routine for years now and still have "code brown" days, but Dan copes with all aspects of it amazingly well. It is such a blessing that he is not distressed by any of it.

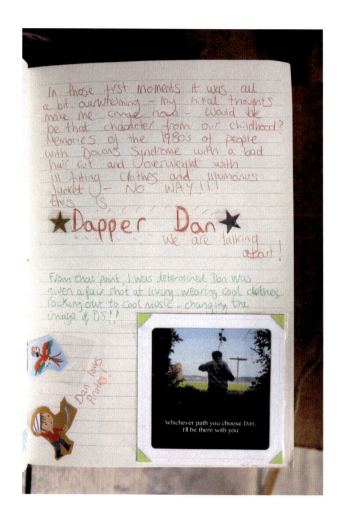

Early memories of Dan include being stopped everywhere we went because of his incredible amount of hair! We had a positive initial experience and embraced that "proud new parent" feeling. It was heaven.

Mark:

We always had wonderful support from our family and close friends, and if anything, the appearance of Dan has drawn us all closer and made us happier people.

Karena:

The early years did have some isolating times. I found it difficult to make friends with people who had babies or little ones the same age as mine. All my current friends were not ready for their own families yet, but I think being a mum at only twenty-three did help. I was naive and

lived in blissful ignorance to a degree. I didn't worry about what the future held. I just enjoyed the experience and concentrated on working with Dan at our local children's center to help him achieve his next milestone.

Mark:

In February 2005, Dan's sister, Eve, was welcomed into the world. During the pregnancy, we opted for the Chorionic Villus Sampling (CVS) test. We both felt we needed to know and prepare ourselves for what awaited us at birth. After the unexpected news when Dan was born, we felt we needed to be better prepared.

In the spring, at a routine test, it was discovered that Eve had a congenital heart defect called Pulmonary Valve Stenosis which required microsurgery at six months. This was a success and she is now being monitored every two years, so all is well.

Karena:

Dan attends a special school due to his learning delay being assessed as severe. We feel he receives the best possible learning opportunities and experiences.

Mark:

He loves the school as we all do, and his social activities are extended to after school clubs and spending more quality time with friends.

He really enjoys watching his local football team, of which he's been a mascot on several occasions. They have taken him in as the twelfth man on the pitch, awarding him with football shirts. One opposing team even gave him a signed football!

One real love of his is disco dancing. Wherever we are, wherever there's a dance floor, that's where he'll be! First on, last off – every time!

... brown ... days but Do
ges with all aspects of it amaz
— it is such a blessing that he
distressed by any of it

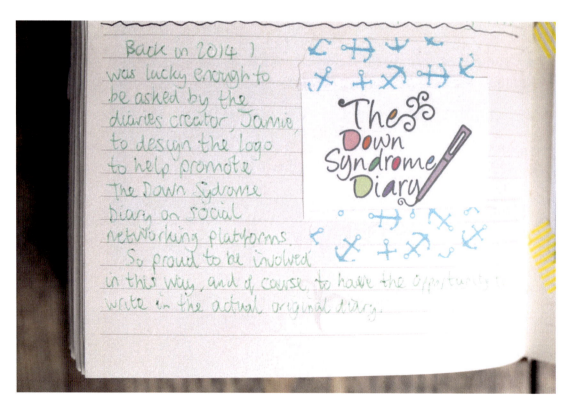

Back in 2014 I
was lucky enough to
be asked by the
diaries creator, Jamie,
to design the logo
to help promote
The Down Sydrome
Diary on social
networking platforms.
So proud to be involved
in this way, and of course, to have the opportunity
write in the actual original diary.

The Down Syndrome Diary

Dan has a more star-studded life than any other family member, appearing in a TV show in the UK called "Something Special," which is predominately for children with learning disabilities. He spent the whole day filming with Justin Fletch in 2010 (those in the UK will know who this is). Even now, we get messages from friends telling us his episode has been repeated again!

Back in 2014, I was lucky enough to be asked by the diary's creator, Jamie, to design the logo to help promote *The Down Syndrome Diary* on social networking platforms. I was so proud to be involved in this way, and of course to have the opportunity to write in the original diary.

Eve:

Hi, this is Eve, Dan's sister. I'm 13. As Dan is three years older than me, I have grown up with him since the beginning. Dan is the best brother I could ever imagine having, but sometimes it's hard.

Dan began to lose his speech six years ago. He can only speak simple words with some additional signing. As Dan is unable to communicate easily, in the holidays it can get quite lonely.

However, Dan having Down's Syndrome has taught me so many things that I wouldn't have learnt without him. I remember when I was younger, me and my friend would get out the big packs of Dan's nappies and make stepping stones and forts out of them. We had so much fun! Not every kid gets to do that!

Dan struggles with some things that I help out with such as speaking, making breakfast, etc.

Having a brother like Dan has made me want to get a job working with children with disabilities and illnesses. I would love to do play therapy as I love to see their smiles.

My friends are all very understanding and supportive, even though I have received some negative attitude from people in my class that I try to ignore. Dan has made me understand that it's ok. In fact, it's fantastic to be different, and I love him in every possible way!

Mark:

Dan makes a very positive impact on everyone he meets, especially his immediate family. His arrival prompted me to raise awareness for the Down's Syndrome community. It was suggested that a Google Doodle proposal should be designed to do just that. The doodles appear on Google's homepage to commemorate special days throughout the year. So I set about designing one for World Down Syndrome Day, which is 21st March, every year.

I campaigned for this on Facebook and Twitter with the tireless help of many others, and for a number of years with no luck. So I worked on designing something different – a stand alone image for social networkers to share. Wendy and Mike O'Carroll, who are also featured in the diary, suggested a photoshoot for families holding the image, to mark World Down Syndrome Day in 2016.

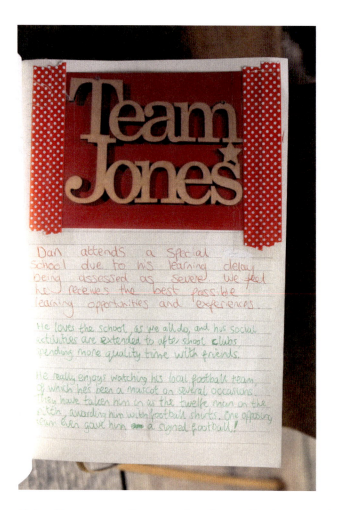

Dan attends a special school due to his learning delay being assessed as severe. We feel he receives the best possible learning opportunities and experiences.

He loves the school, as we all do, and his social activities are extended to after school clubs spending more quality time with friends.

He really enjoys watching his local football team of which he's been a mascot on several occasions. They have taken him on as the twelfe man on the pitch, awarding him with football shirts. One opposing team even gave him a signed football!

Karena:

Although Dan is a smiley and cooperative young man, he has undergone one concerning change over the last five years… he has gradually lost his speech.

This loss has been so gradual that for the first two years we did not notice until we watched an old home video. Unfortunately, getting answers as to why this happened has been a long road. It has been blamed on his hearing, being lazy, being a teenager, etc… but as a mum, you just know something is not right. Dan was becoming withdrawn. Tests eventually indicated that Dan was Vitamin D deficient and this has helped a little in bringing some of our old Dan back. However, later tests diagnosed him ASD (Autism).

We are also currently looking into anxiety as a possible explanation for his "not talking." This is unusual, but several things are now indicating this. Dan recently surprised us all when we tried "facilitated communication" (Google this) out of desperation and found that he can read and type with hand support. This has opened up our world to him again!

We continue our journey to support, advocate, and cheerlead Dan in all parts of his life as he moves towards adulthood – teaching him life skills and looking forward to it being his round at the pub!

Stay Strong.

Team Jones X

Keep up with Team Jones on Twitter – @jonertweets and on Instagram @jonergram

We continue our Journey to support, advocate and cheerlead Dan in all parts of his life as he moves towards adulthood - Teaching him life skills and looking forward to it being his round at the pub!

Stay Strong!

Team Jones X

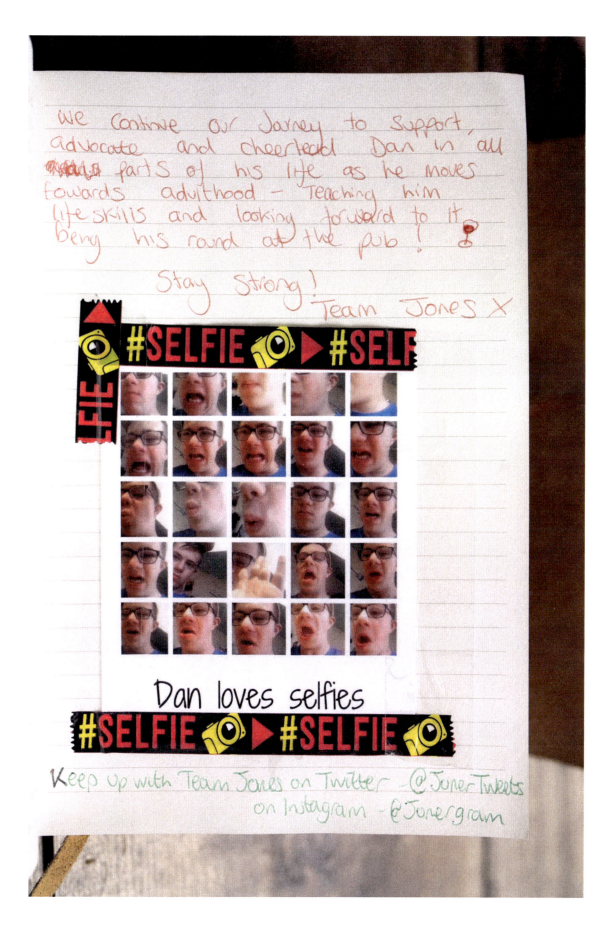

Keep up with Team Jones on Twitter - @JonesTweets
on Instagram - @Jonesgram

Claire-May Minett

"So please, if you meet a person with Down syndrome, sit down, talk to them and actively listen to what they have to say. We bring so much 'extra' to this world."

—Claire-May Minett

Claire-May Minett
Manchester
North West England

Thursday November 8, 2018

My name is Claire-May Minett, I am forty years old and you're probably thinking that I am just another parent. But I am not just anyone. I am unique and very rare in England. I have been staring at a box that looks just like a Christmas present, but instead it is the box that has this diary inside. I want to share my experiences with you and give you an exclusive and different perspective for the last entry. There are three types of Down syndrome – Trisomy 21, Translocation, and Mosaic. I myself have Mosaic Down syndrome.

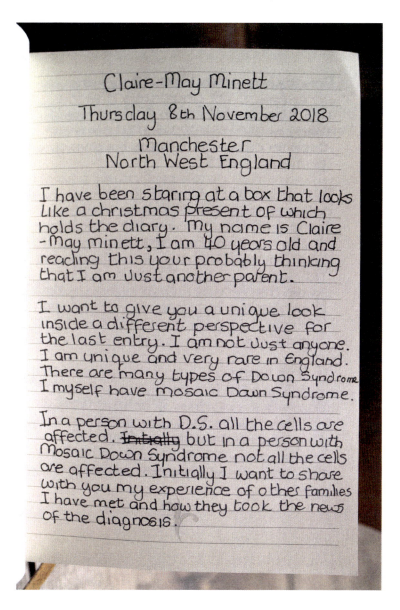

Did you know that in the UK every year, approximately four percent of babies are born with Down syndrome, but only two percent of those babies have the Mosaic variety? Society has come a long way in terms of accepting people who are different. Yet there is still room for improvement.

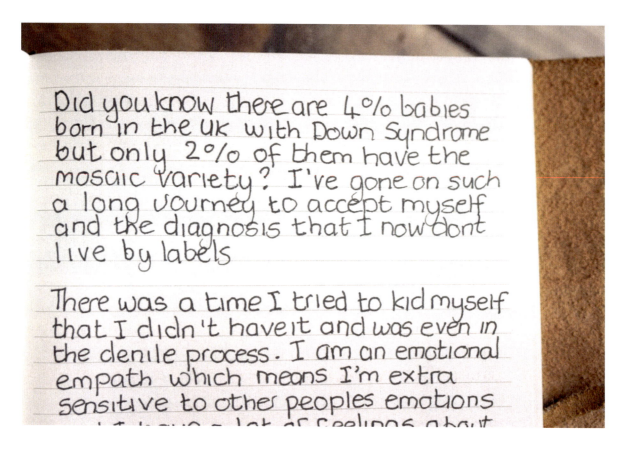

Families can now receive a diagnosis of Down syndrome before birth with various types of genetic testing. But when I was born in August of 1978, there wasn't a lot of information about Down syndrome. Back then, there was no community awareness and no Internet to search for or gather information from. My mother didn't know or understand that I was different. It was years later when she noticed that my traits and behaviours were different. In 1989, when I was ten years old, my mother learned that I had Mosaic Down syndrome. There was no support and no services in our area for a child like me. In fact, we lived in a village where there was only myself and another girl named Katherine who had Down syndrome. At the time, the headmaster of my primary school told my mother not to go looking for support because there wasn't any.

I grew up in an artistic family. My grandfather was a local artist (painter) and my mother followed in his footsteps. My brother also took to the arts and could play a number of instruments. My interest in the arts came in the form of dance. I started off performing at a young age and took dance lessons at "Turners," a local dance organization in our area.

(me as a Turners dancer)

I went on to perform with the Church Players amateur drama group, and then to musical theatre until the time came when my mom pushed me into the "world of work." Although it took several years, I learned and understood how to work and behave professionally in the workplace. Despite my efforts and the fact that I am wise beyond my years, I was immediately discriminated against (that's a different story altogether), so I returned to school to learn something I was quite passionate about. I attended College and received a BTEC in Media Studies, and then achieved a university media degree. I am now working and volunteering as a freelance filmmaker/editor, and I'm a huge film buff with a keen interest in the media industry. I love being on TV, and have appeared on a couple of reality shows and online content, but I am still learning and working at enhancing my acting skills. I have also worked at BBC, Nine Lives, and at a production house.

I also got married in 2000, but we later divorced in 2006. During that time, I did volunteer work and supported families of children with disabilities, including those with Mosaic Down syndrome. I learned so much and became a self-advocate. In 2011, I was asked to speak at an event for the International Mosaic Down Syndrome Association. I immediately said yes because it gave me a chance to tell my story and connect with others like myself. I also wanted to attend because they are based in the United States of America and I love the country! Because of that event, I now have some amazing friends whom I love dearly.

There was a time when I was in denial about my diagnosis and I tried to convince myself that I didn't have Down syndrome. It has been a long journey for me to accept myself and my diagnosis. I have my struggles and issues just like anyone else. People with Mosaic Down syndrome are prone to depression which explains my "yo-yo" moods. I'm also an emotional empath which means I am extra sensitive to other people's emotions. Through the conferences I've attended and the connections I've made, I've developed the confidence to be myself no matter what! Although I have come a long way, I know that there is still room for improvement in so many different areas of my life.

Due to my diagnosis, my development has always been a bit behind but that didn't stop or hinder my determination to be a success in life. I live my life fully and don't live by labels. I have done and achieved things you couldn't imagine a person with Down syndrome actually doing. This is the main reason why I'm an inspiration to many within the community. Those of us in the Down syndrome community can enrich the lives of others by creating awareness and lifting the stigma of ignorance. We bring an extra chromosome and an extra talent to the world! For instance, I have a friend, Eva-Grace, who is absolutely amazing! She is only four years old but she has a recurring role as a character in the popular Chester Soap "Hollyoaks."

(me as a teenage dancer)

I am me and I am here to prove not just to my community but to everyone, that people with Down syndrome are strong-willed and can do things just like anyone else. It just may take a bit longer to achieve it. Although I fight for what is right for my Down Syndrome community, the society in England is still so far behind (I'm a bit of an anti-nationalist and have strong feelings about the UK). I know people are more accepting of differences, but just wait until you come face to face with that "clique" of people who can't see past the nose on their face!

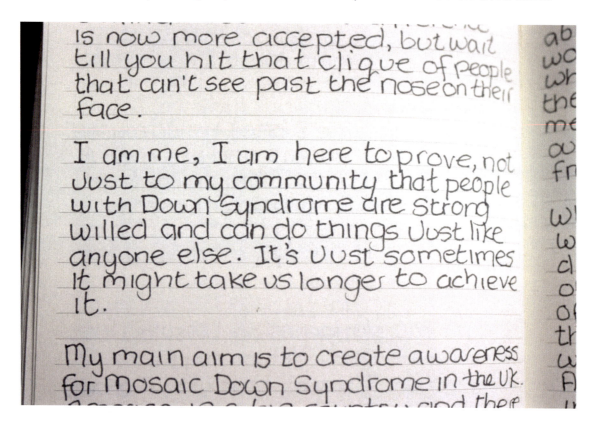

Ultimately, my main goal is to create awareness for Mosaic Down Syndrome in the UK. The US seems to have more awareness, perhaps because they are a larger country, but I am still fighting for it here at home. It has been frustrating at times but I persevere. I also give back to the community by participating in research studies on Down syndrome. This year, I presented at the World Down Syndrome Congress, which was held in Glasgow, Scotland. I ran into many people I knew from the Down syndrome community, but I also had the opportunity to meet others from all around the world. It was the most amazing experience. My experiences have taught me so much and I now have a broad awareness of the world around me

Medical professionals are now more experienced and seemingly more "in tune" when delivering news to their patients. However, in the world of Down syndrome, this is a different matter. Some families I have met had doctors and physicians who used positive and encouraging words when delivering the diagnosis. However, other parents I've spoken to were given more negative information and were told, "I'm sorry but your child has Down syndrome." If it were me, I would not be sorry. Instead, I would be doing cartwheels down the corridor! I believe that children with Down syndrome are given to those who want more from life, and who will challenge others to see differing perspectives.Some people also say that children with Down syndrome are "angels" and a "blessing from God." I don't debate this belief but I also know and understand that every child is unique.

So please, if you meet a person with Down syndrome, sit down, talk to them and actively listen to what they have to say. We bring so much "extra" to this world. Without us, the world would have no hugs. Think of it as embracing the world and bringing love back to the human race. Let's face it, there is a lack of empathy in these times and we all need some love in our lives. Expose yourself to different people and experience everything you can. Don't live just by your means. Push yourself out of your comfort zone. The world isn't scary. Believe in yourself and help others! You are amazing!

Thank you for reading.

Claire-May Minett
Finished entry 22.11.18

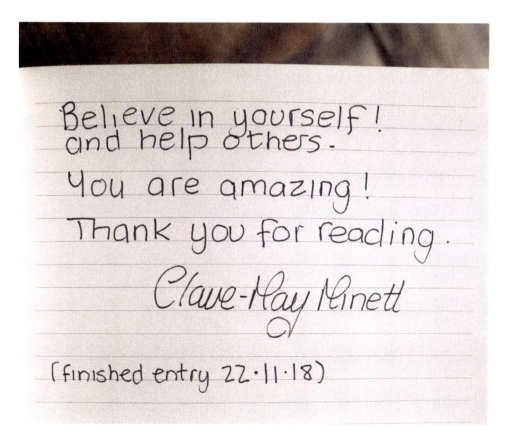

Afterword

And so the diary found its way back home in the Winter of 2020...

So, now what? What's next? Where do we go from here?

My friends... we keep on advocating, we keep on celebrating, and most of all we keep on loving every minute of this life we've all been blessed with.

And when it gets hard, because it will get hard, please remember that your friends are right inside these pages and here to hold you through anything that comes your way.

Acknowledgement

I don't even know to begin saying thank you to everyone that helped see this project through, but I'm going to try my best.

Chelsea Rebeck – our fearless legal guru! You are amazing, and I am beyond thankful for all your help since day 1.

Sara Demick – Thank you for your tireless efforts photographing every single page at just the right angle to attempt to capture the soul of this diary in print. You are an amazing photographer, and I'm honored to know you.

Kelly Searle – Thank you for putting the diary through its first photoshoot and giving me so many beautiful images to promote it with through the years!

Carla Shaw – Thank you, my lifelong friend, for all the nights you spent typing up entries for us. Love you lots!

Christine DeFroy – You never ceased to ask me what I needed help with despite your unimaginable workload with your babies. I love you dearly!

Mark Jones – Thank you for all your work through the years on our amazing logo, frames, and pretty much anything I needed help with.

Hugh Gall – Thank you for working so hard on the upcoming documentary and video work you're doing to continue telling our story.

Elizabeth Lewis – Thank you for your support and all your help with the cover. It's truly beautiful!

Tami Spence, Taylor Capps, Belinda Mendes, Jessica Firman, Jackie Weldon, Julie Jones Bailey, and Nikki Dockery – Thank you for being my editing team!

Katie Goncalves – Thank you for the massive task of editing the full manuscript!

Mom, Stace, Tam, MaryAnne, Aimee & Erin – Thank you for always being my biggest cheerleaders!

Ramie – You know why! You keep me sane...

Bobby & Delly – Thank you for loving Benny like he was your own son since day 1. He is so lucky to have his Abuelito & Lola in his life!

Dad – Thank you for saying the most perfect thing you ever could have possibly said when I told you Benny would be born with Down syndrome... "So what?"

Mark – Thank you for putting up with a wife that is determined to publish a book, excel at a full-time job, be supermom to three amazing kiddos, and about a handful of other things at any given time. I can't do what I do without you doing what you do behind the scenes. You are an amazing father and husband, and I love that I get to spend my life with you.

Ellie & Norah – Thank you for being the best sisters I could have ever imagined for Benny.

And to all the other family and friends throughout my life that love me, support me, and help me through, I hope you know what you mean to me. I don't know what I did to deserve such an amazing village, but I sure am glad I have each and every one of you!

xoxo – Jamie

Glossary

Almond Eyes

Almond shaped eyes with an upward slant are a common physical trait of individuals with Down syndrome.

Amniocentesis

Amniocentesis is a medical procedure used primarily in prenatal diagnosis of chromosomal abnormalities and fetal infections as well as for sex determination

Apnea (Sleep)

Sleep Apnea is an often serious condition where the individual stops and starts breathing throughout the night. A common procedure to test for this is called a "Sleep Study" and is recommended for all children with Down syndrome. According to NDSS.org, there is a 50-100% incidence of obstructive sleep apnea in individuals with Down Syndrome, with almost 60% of children with Down syndrome having abnormal sleep studies by age 3.5 – 4 years. The overall incidence of obstructive sleep apnea increases as children grow older.

ASD (Autism Spectrum Disorder)

A developmental disorder that impairs the individual's ability to communicate and interact with others. According to NDSS.org, an Autism diagnosis has been identified in somewhere between five and seven percent of individuals with Down syndrome.

ASD (Atrial Septal Defect)

A congenital heart condition that happens when a hole is identified between the top two chambers of the heart. According to GlobalDownSyndrome.org, approximately 50% of children born with Down syndrome will also have a congenital heart defect such as ASD.

ASL (American Sign Language)

American Sign Language is a natural language that serves as the predominant sign language of Deaf communities in the United States and most of Anglophone Canada. In the United States. It is common for babies with Down syndrome to learn sign language as their speech is often delayed.

Auditory Processing Disorder

A disorder affecting the ability to understand speech.

AVDS (Atrial Ventricular Septal Defect)

A congenital heart condition that happens when a hole is identified between the bottom two chambers of the heart. According to GlobalDownSyndrome.org, approximately 50% of children born with Down syndrome will also have a congenital heart defect such as ASD.

Bicuspid Aortic Valve

Some people with Down syndrome are born with a bicuspid aortic valve, in which the aortic valve – located between the lower left heart chamber (left ventricle) and the main artery that leads to the body (aorta) – has only two (bicuspid) cusps instead of three.

C-PTSD

Complex post-traumatic stress disorder (C-PTSD; also known as complex trauma disorder) is a psychological disorder that can develop in response to prolonged, repeated experience of interpersonal trauma in a context in which the individual has little or no chance of escape.

Cannula

A thin tube inserted into a vein or body cavity to administer medicine, drain off fluid, or insert a surgical instrument.

CHD (Congenital Heart Disease)

Congenital heart disease is one or more problems with the heart's structure that exist since birth. Congenital means that you're born with the defect. Congenital heart disease, also called congenital heart defect, can change the way blood flows through your heart. According to NDSS.org, approximately 50% of babies born with Down syndrome have a CHD.

Complete AV Canal Defect / AV Canal Complete

Complete atrioventricular canal (CAVC) is a severe congenital heart disease in which there is a large hole in the tissue (the septum) that separates the left and right sides of the heart. The hole is in the center of the heart, where the upper chambers (the atria) and the lower chambers (the ventricles) meet.

Congenital Cataracts

A congenital cataract is a clouding of the eye's natural lens that is present at birth.

Croup

Croup refers to an infection of the upper airway, which obstructs breathing and causes a characteristic barking cough.

CVS Chorionic Villus Sampling

Chorionic villus sampling, sometimes called "chorionic villous sampling", is a form of prenatal diagnosis to determine chromosomal or genetic disorders in the fetus.

Early Intervention Therapy

Is the term used to describe the services and supports that are available to babies and young children with developmental delays and disabilities and their families.

ECHO/Echocardiogram (FETAL)

An echocardiogram (echo) is a graphic outline of the heart's movement. During an echo test, ultrasound (high-frequency sound waves) from a hand-held wand placed on your chest provides pictures of the heart's valves and chambers and helps the sonographer evaluate the pumping action of the heart. A fetal echo is done in utero.

EKG

An electrocardiogram (ECG or EKG) records the electrical signal from your heart to check for different heart conditions. Electrodes are placed on your chest to record your heart's electrical signals, which cause your heart to beat.

Endocrinologist

Endocrinologists are doctors who specialize in glands and the hormones they make. They deal with metabolism, or all the biochemical processes that make your body work, including how your body changes food into energy and how it grows. Thyroid function is often an issue with individuals with Down syndrome, and therefore an endocrinologist may be needed.

ENT Doctor

Ear, nose & throat specialist. These doctors are essential for individuals with Down syndrome due to the smaller nature of their sinuses and ear canals, as well as their proclivity to having obstructive sleep apnea.

Facilitated Communication

Facilitated communication is a technique that involves a facilitator physically supporting the hand, wrist or arm of an autistic person while the person spells out words on a keyboard or similar device. It's sometimes called 'assisted typing' or 'supported typing'.

Failure To Thrive

Failure to thrive (FTT) is slow physical development in a baby or child. This is commonly found in individuals with Down syndrome during childhood or beyond.

Fetal Heart Specialist

Fetal cardiologists are pediatric cardiologists who have special expertise in the diagnosis and management of problems that affect a baby's heart, both before and after birth. There are a number of reasons for your doctor to ask you to see a fetal cardiologist.

G-Tube

Some kids with Down syndrome have trouble getting enough nutrition by mouth. A gastrostomy tube (also called a G-tube) is a tube inserted through the belly that brings nutrition directly to the stomach. It's one of the ways doctors can make sure kids who have trouble eating get the fluid and calories they need.

Genetic Counselor

Genetic counselors check family medical history and medical records, order genetic tests, evaluate the results of these tests and records, and help parents understand what all of it means. Genetic tests are done by analyzing small samples of blood or body tissues. They determine whether you, your partner, or your baby carry genes for some inherited disorders. If your child has Down syndrome, this can be useful to determine which type of Down syndrome they have: Trisomy 21, Translocation, or Mosaic.

Heart Murmur

According to mayclinic.com, heart murmurs are sounds – such as whooshing or swishing – made by turbulent blood in or near your heart.

Hirschsprung's Disease

According to mayclinic.com, Hirschsprung's disease is a condition that affects the large intestine (colon) and causes problems with passing stool. The condition is present at birth (congenital) as a result of missing nerve cells in the muscles of the baby's colon. According to NDSS.org, this affects between 2-15% of babies born with Down syndrome.

Hyperthyroidism

According to mayclinic.com, Hyperthyroidism (overactive thyroid) occurs when your thyroid gland produces too much of the hormone thyroxine. Hyperthyroidism can accelerate your body's metabolism, causing unintentional weight loss and a rapid or irregular heartbeat. Thyroid issues are common in individuals with Down syndrome.

Hypothyroidism

According to mayclinic.com, Hypothyroidism (underactive thyroid) is a condition in which your thyroid gland doesn't produce enough of certain crucial hormones. Hypothyroidism may not cause noticeable symptoms in the early stages. Thyroid issues are common in individuals with Down syndrome.

Hypotonia

According to surestep.net, hypotonia is the decreased level of muscle tone. It leaves your child's muscles feeling too relaxed. That's why kids with low tone are sometimes compared to ragdolls. Side note, this is also the reason EVERYONE loves holding a baby with Down syndrome… they melt right into you! All babies with Down syndrome are born with varying levels of hypotonia.

Imperforate Anus

According to rarediseases.org, Imperforate anus is a rare inborn abnormality characterized by the absence or abnormal localization of the anus.

Jaundice

According to kidshealth.org, babies with jaundice have a yellow coloring of the skin and eyes. This happens when there is too much bilirubin in the baby's blood.

Lactation Consultant

A consultant that works with new mother's that would like to breastfeed their newborns. Lactation consultants are very helpful for a newborn with Down syndrome as they often having difficult latching due to hypotonia.

Leukemia

According to WebMD.com, Childhood leukemia, the most common type of cancer in children and teens, is a cancer of the white blood cells. Abnormal white blood cells form in the bone marrow. They quickly travel through the bloodstream and crowd out healthy cells. This raises the body's chances of infection and other problems. According to NDSS.org, Down syndrome is a risk factor for childhood leukemia.

Makaton Sign Language

According to singinghands.co.uk, Makaton signs are based on the gestures used in BSL (British Sign Language – the language of the Deaf community). However, unlike BSL, Makaton signs are used in conjunction with speech at all times and in English grammatical word order. With Makaton, children and adults can communicate using signs and symbols.

Mosaic Down Syndrome

According to IMDSA.org, mosaicism means that some cells of the body have trisomy 21, and some have the typical number of chromosomes.

NICU (Neonatal Intensive Care Unit)

Many babies born with down syndrome spend some time in the NICU for various issues associated with Down syndrome.

NG (Nasogastric) Tube

According to verywellhealth.com, a nasogastric (NG) tube is a flexible tube of rubber or plastic that is passed through the nose, down through the esophagus, and into the stomach. It can be used to either remove substances from or add them to the stomach. An NG tube is only meant to be used on a temporary basis and is not for long-term use.

Non-Invasive Prenatal Testing (NIPT)

According to medlineplus.gov, Noninvasive prenatal testing (NIPT), sometimes called noninvasive prenatal screening (NIPS), is a method of determining the risk that the fetus will be born with certain genetic abnormalities. This testing analyzes small fragments of DNA that are circulating in a pregnant woman's blood.

Orthotic Helmet

According to healthychildren.org, helmet therapy (also called helmet orthosis) is a treatment that's prescribed to help mold the baby's skull into shape. An Orthotic Helmet would be the type of helmet used in this type of therapy. This is a very common therapy needed by babies with Down syndrome as they tend not to move their heads around too much during sleep.

OT (Occupational Therapy)

According to aota.org, occupational therapy practitioners work with persons with Down syndrome to help them master skills for independence through self-care like feeding and dressing, fine and gross motor skills, school performance, and play and leisure activities.

Palmar Crease

A somewhat commonly occurring trait associated with Down syndrome and other genetic conditions, a Palmar Crease is a single deep crease across the center of the palm. It is also referred to as a Simian Crease.

PT (Physical Therapy)

Physical therapists well versed in Down syndrome are a crucial part of therapy programs starting at birth. They can assist the individual with Down syndrome in developing Gross Motor Skills to help with everything from crawling to walking and beyond. Ensuring the PT understands hypotonia and ligament laxity as these commonly occur in Down syndrome.

PVS (Pulmonary Vein Stenosis)

According to pubmed.gov, Pulmonary vein stenosis (PVS) is a rare and serious cardiovascular condition in which oxygenated blood from the lungs cannot easily return to the left side of the heart to be pumped out of the body.

Pulmonary Valve Stenosis

Pulmonary stenosis is a congenital (present at birth) defect that occurs due to abnormal development of the prenatal heart during the first eight weeks of pregnancy.

Quad Screen

According to healthline.com, the quad screen – also called the maternal serum screen – is a prenatal screening test that analyzes four substances in your blood. It's usually carried out between your 15th and 22nd week of pregnancy. This test can detect if you are potentially high-risk for Down syndrome, and would lead to further testing if you chose to do so.

Small Nose

A lack of a nasal bone is a powerful marker for Down syndrome. This marker can be detected on an ultrasound or at birth. It also results in the cutest button nose you could ever see on a baby!

Soft Markers

According to radiopedia.org, antenatal soft ultrasound markers are fetal sonographic findings that are generally not abnormalities as such but are indicative of an increased age adjusted risk of an underlying fetal aneuploidic or some non chromosomal abnormalities. Essentially, there are things they can see on an ultrasound that could possibly diagnose the presence of Down syndrome IF there are multiple markers. For instance, a short femur alone would be a soft marker, but wouldn't be cause for recommending further testing unless there was also a congenital heart defect suspected.

Speech (Shortened for Speech Therapy)

According to NDSS.org, children with Down syndrome have strengths and challenges in development of communication skills, including receptive (understanding) language and expressive (speaking and composing sentences) language skills and reading. It takes a team to help children and adolescents progress well in speech and language; that team typically includes speech-language pathologists, physicians, classroom teachers, special educators and families. Speech-language pathologists have information and expertise to help address the speech and language problems faced by many children with Down syndrome.

SRB (Specialist Resource Base)

Specialist Resource Bases refers to the programme of additionally commissioned services funded from the High Needs Block and delivered by schools. The service is for learners with a high level of special educational needs who are educated in mainstream schools in the UK.

T&A (Tonsils & Adenoids)

Tonsils- small masses of lymphoid tissue in the throat

TBI

Traumatic brain injury

Tetralogy of Fallot

A congenital heart defect with four abnormalities at once.

Tongue Thrust

The tongue presses forward too far in the mouth causing the appearance of the tongue between the teeth. This is normally due to trouble breathing through the nose and low muscle tone in people with Down syndrome.

Translocation Down Syndrome

Translocation Down syndrome is a type of Down syndrome that is caused when one chromosome breaks off and attaches to another chromosome. In this case, there are three 21 chromosomes but one of the 21 chromosomes is attached to another chromosome.

Trisomy-21

The most common form of Down syndrome. A second copy of the 21st chromosome.

White spot or echogenic intracardiac foci on heart during ultrasound

A bright spot seen on a baby's heart during an ultrasound. These are small deposits of calcium and most of the time do not cause any harm. Although it could be the detection of a heart defect for children with Down syndrome.

Resources

For further information and support for families raising children with Down syndrome, please visit the following organizations:

Down Syndrome Diagnosis Network: www.dsdiagnosisnetwork.org

Global Down Syndrome Foundation: http://www.globaldownsyndrome.org

Down Syndrome International: www.ds-int.org

International Down Syndrome Coalition: http://theidsc.org/

International Mosaic Down Syndrome Association: http://www.imdsa.org/

European Down Syndrome Association (EDSA): http://www.edsa.eu/

National Down Syndrome Society (NDSS): http://www.ndss.org

Thank You to all my writers, my friends…

Tara, Helen, Amy, Steve, Kelly, Kimberly, Crystal, Holly, Mallory, Crystal H, Angela, Meriah, Karen, Patricia, Chelsey, Christine, Abigail, Michelle, Wendy, Mike, Hayley, Wyn, Megan, Erik, Vicky, Karena, Mark & Claire…

WE DID IT!

Made in the USA
Las Vegas, NV
27 June 2021